111 ChatGPT AI Prompts
for Leadership, Coaching & Mentoring
to Boost Your Business Career

111 ChatGPT AI Prompts

for Leadership, Coaching & Mentoring
to Boost Your Business Career

Increase Insights & Career Growth with AI-Powered Leadership Prompts Suitable to ChatGPT, Copilot, **Gemini** & Llama

Mindscape Artwork Publishing
Mauricio Vasquez

Toronto, Canada

Authors:
Mauricio Vasquez

First Printing: November 2023

ISBN-978-1-990709-88-3 (Paperback)

ISBN-978-1-998402-15-1 (Hardcover)

DEDICATION

To the committed professionals and future leaders striving for excellence: Consider this book your toolkit, supplying you with the essential skills and wisdom to excel in an increasingly complex work environment.

INTRODUCTION

Welcome to an unparalleled guide that fuses classical principles in mentoring, coaching, and leadership with the revolutionary scope of Generative Artificial Intelligence (AI). Authored by Mauricio Vasquez, an expert in coaching, leadership, and AI-based strategies, this book is an indispensable asset for professionals desiring a transformative impact in their respective fields.

As professionals navigate an increasingly intricate and volatile landscape, this book furnishes you with actionable, data-supported insights. Leveraging the capabilities of Generative AI, the book transcends mere theoretical discussions, aiming for measurable, real-world impact tailored to your unique professional environment. Here, Generative AI is not merely an add-on; it's an integral framework. This guide embraces its adaptive capabilities, illustrating how AI can customize guidance, stimulate inventive thinking, and serve as a catalyst for effective and meaningful professional interactions.

The objective of the book is unambiguous: to amplify your professional skill set across multiple dimensions. Whether you are entering the workforce, an established leader, or someone open to innovative practices, this book provides an enriching blend of practicality and adaptability.

Going beyond the introduction of methodologies and tools, this book endeavors to recalibrate your foundational thinking around professional influence and leadership. Expect an in-depth dive into crafting compelling narratives, fine-tuning AI-driven prompts, and mastering the mechanics of impactful professional relations.

Prepare to embark on a transformative journey towards achieving an unmatched level of professional efficacy and societal impact. Welcome to the vanguard of meaningful, sustainable professional development.

ABOUT THE AUTHOR

Mauricio Vasquez is a multifaceted professional with over 20 years of experience in risk management and insurance, specializing in sectors like mining, power, and renewable energy. He holds an Industrial Engineering degree, a Master's in Business Administration, and a Master's in Marketing and Commercial Management, along with certifications in Enterprise Risk Management and Artificial Intelligence.

Mauricio is also a certified Adler Trained Coach and a self-published author, focusing on personal growth and professional development. His expertise in Artificial Intelligence and Large Language Models Prompt engineering adds a unique layer to his professional background. Fluent in both English and Spanish, Mauricio has worked across Canada, the U.S., Latin America, and the Caribbean. In addition to his corporate roles, he is a Professional and Life Coach, committed to helping immigrants transition successfully to new lives in Canada. His approach is deeply rooted in building long-term relationships and providing tailored, impactful solutions to clients.

If you want to connect with Mauricio, go to this link
https://www.linkedin.com/in/mauriciovasquez or scan this QR code:

WHAT IS GENERATIVE ARTIFICIAL INTELLIGENCE (AI)?

In the vanguard of Artificial Intelligence (AI), Generative AI is not just another milestone; it is an entire saga rewriting the rules of what AI can accomplish. This is not a marginal refinement in data analytics. It's artificial intelligence capable of generating text, images, or other media, using generative models.

Conventional AI excels at dissecting and interpreting existing data. Generative AI, on the other hand, elevates this by generating entirely original, value-infused content. From crafting compelling emails to architecting strategic initiatives and enhancing coaching dialogues, Generative AI amplifies human capabilities while fundamentally redefining avenues for inventive solutions.

Anchored in sophisticated neural network architectures, Generative AI transcends basic mimicry to understand and extrapolate intricate human behavioral patterns. The scope of its impact is staggering, pervading diverse sectors such as marketing dynamics, C-suite leadership, and even personal self-actualization. This is not a theoretical marvel confined to the lab; it's an applied innovation with practical, immediate, and far-reaching implications.

As we pivot to the forthcoming chapter, with a focus on Natural Language Processing (NLP) Chatbots, recognize that Generative AI serves as the bedrock of these advanced conversational platforms. Within the realms of coaching, mentoring, and transformative leadership, it is Generative AI that enriches these chatbots, enabling them to produce not just relevant but deeply contextual and emotionally nuanced dialogues. The result? An elevated coaching paradigm supplemented by data-driven, yet profoundly human-like insights. To ignore the capabilities of Generative AI is to forego the boundless opportunities for innovation and enhanced efficacy it unreservedly offers.

WHAT ARE NATURAL LANGUAGE PROCESSING CHATBOTS?

An Artificial Intelligence (AI) Chatbot is a program within a website or app that uses machine learning (ML) and natural language processing (NLP) to interpret inputs and understand the intent behind a request or "prompt" (more on this later in the book). Chatbots can be rule-based with simple use cases or more advanced and able to handle multiple conversations.

The rise of language models like GPT has revolutionized the landscape of conversational AI. These Chatbots now boast advanced capabilities that can mimic not just a human conversation style but also a (super) human mind. They can find information online and produce unique content and insights.

The most important thing to know about an AI Chatbot is that it combines ML and NLP to understand what people need and bring the best answers. Some AI Chatbots are better for personal use, like conducting research, and others are best for business use, like featuring a Chatbot on your company's website.

With this in mind, we've compiled a list of the best AI Chatbots at the time of the writing of this book. We strongly suggest that you try and test each of the most popular ones and see what works best for you.

ChatGPT:
- Uses NLP to understand the context of conversations to provide related and original responses in a human-like conversation.

- Multiple use cases for things like answering questions, ideating and getting inspiration, or generating new content [like a marketing email].
- Improves over time as it has more conversations.

Microsoft Copilot/Bing Chat:
- Uses NLP and ML to understand conversation prompts.
- The compose feature can generate original written content and images, and its powerful search engine capabilities can surface answers from the web.
- It's a conversational tool, so you can continue sending messages until you're satisfied.

Google Gemini/Bard:
- Google's Bard is a multi-use AI Chatbot.
- It's powered by Google's LaMDA [instead of GPT].
- Use it for things like brainstorming and ideation, drafting unique and original content, or getting answers to your questions.
- Connected to Google's website index so it can access information from the internet.

Meta LLaMa:
- Meta's Chatbot is an open source large language [LLM].
- The tool is trained using reinforcement learning from human feedback [RLHF], learning from the preferences and ratings of human AI trainers.

Starting from now, we will refer to these platforms as Chatbots. For a guide on how to sign up to each, please refer to Appendix No 1.

If you're seeking a beginner-friendly, step-by-step guide to using ChatGPT, please refer to Appendix No. 3. This appendix includes access to our report, "Elevate Your Productivity Using ChatGPT," which offers a detailed guide on leveraging ChatGPT to boost efficiency and productivity across a range of professional environments.

As of the book's publication date, the information herein is current and accurate. The Chatbot industry, however, is dynamic, with constant updates and new entrants. While specifics may evolve, our prompts, core strategies and principles discussed in this book are designed to withstand the test of time, offering you a robust framework for navigating this fast-paced landscape.

THE BENEFITS OF USING AI CHATBOTS IN YOUR COACHING, MENTORING AND LEADERSHIP JOURNEY

In today's complex professional landscape, effective leadership, coaching, and mentorship require a dynamic skill set that can feel like a job in and of itself. Enter Chatbots and conversational agents like ChatGPT, game-changing technologies that are becoming invaluable allies for professionals in these fields.

These AI-driven tools are becoming invaluable assets in the realm of professional development. They offer real-time coaching, behavioral insights, and actionable strategies, which can be a boon for anyone aiming to climb the corporate ladder or make an impact as a leader.

The advantages of integrating Chatbots and the insights from this book into your leadership journey can be broken down into five key areas:

1. **Efficiency Amplified:** The immediacy with which Chatbots can deliver actionable insights is invaluable. Whether you are crafting a leadership manifesto or preparing for a coaching session, Chatbots help you accelerate the process, thereby enhancing your overall productivity.
2. **Quality, Data-Backed Inputs:** While human intuition and experience are irreplaceable, Chatbots can serve as a reliable first draft for your strategies. Grounded in data analytics and pattern recognition, they can churn out initial recommendations that you can fine-tune according to your unique needs.
3. **Strategic Differentiation:** Customization is pivotal in leadership and coaching. Chatbots, due to their scalability, empower you to personalize your approaches effortlessly. This customized strategy provides a competitive edge that is crucial for achieving success in leadership roles.
4. **Innovation Catalyst:** The capacity of Chatbots to sift through vast datasets enables them to offer innovative yet data-driven suggestions. This infusion of new ideas can revolutionize your existing practices, encouraging a more forward-thinking approach to leadership and coaching.
5. **Enhanced Self-Actualization:** The synergy between this book and Chatbots aims to bolster your self-confidence. Tailored recommendations, predicated on your distinct challenges and opportunities, will not only affirm your capabilities but also point you toward areas for potential growth.

To sum up, the integration of Chatbots and the insights you will get through this book offer an unparalleled arsenal of tools and strategies. This powerful combination has the potential to transform conventional paradigms in leadership, coaching, and mentorship, arming you with the multifaceted skill set required to excel in these intricate roles.

WHAT ARE PROMPTS?

Imagine stepping into a high-stakes negotiation with only half the information—you're likely to miss the mark. Similarly, Chatbots rely on well-crafted prompts to deliver precise and valuable responses.

Prompts serve as the guiding questions, suggestions, or ideas that instruct Chatbots on how and what to respond. But these aren't just any text or phrase; prompts are carefully engineered inputs designed to optimize the Chatbot's output for quality, relevance, and accuracy.

Prompts are suggestions, questions, or ideas for what Chatbots should respond. And for Chatbots to provide a helpful response to their users, they need a thorough prompt with some background information and relevant context. Becoming a solid prompt writer takes time and experience, but there are also some best practices that you can use to see success fairly quickly:

1. **Be precise in your instructions:** when interacting with Chatbots for leadership or coaching tasks, specificity is paramount. Clearly define the tone, scope, and objectives you wish the Chatbot to achieve. For instance, you might say, "Generate a team motivational message that emphasizes the importance of collaboration and aligns with our Q4 targets. Keep the message under 150 words and use a motivational tone."
2. **Integrate contextual information:** the more context you provide, the better Chatbots can tailor their responses. Always include any relevant background information or guidelines. For example, in the case of crafting a message to resolve team conflicts, you may want to append specific issues or arguments that the team is facing.
3. **Segment your interactions:** complex leadership tasks often have multiple components. Break these down into discrete tasks and use individual prompts for each. If you're generating materials for a leadership workshop, you could use separate prompts for the introduction, body, and conclusion segments.
4. **Continuous refinement:** Chatbots provide a valuable starting point but shouldn't replace your own expertise and voice. Use the generated material as a draft that can be further honed and personalized. This ensures that the content aligns with your unique leadership style and the specific needs of your team or mentees.
5. **Employ follow-up prompts:** to get more nuanced advice, use follow-up prompts based on initial outputs. For example, if your first prompt is, "Outline the key principles for effective leadership," a good follow-up could be, "Explain the application of each principle in remote team settings." This sequencing enriches the dialogue and makes the Chatbot's advice more actionable. Check Appendix No 2 for 1100 follow-up prompts you could use, but remember they also need to be tailored to the specific conversation you are having with the Chatbot.

HOW TO USE THIS BOOK?

In the current professional ecosystem, the topics of coaching, mentoring, and leadership are intricate but filled with unprecedented opportunities. This book offers a comprehensive guide for leveraging artificial intelligence, specifically Chatbots, to gain a competitive edge in these sectors. While the content is structured around key frameworks and principles of leadership and coaching, you are encouraged to engage with this book in a non-linear fashion, focusing on areas most relevant to your immediate and long-term objectives.

1. **Optimize your outcomes with our specialized GPT:** We are thrilled to provide exclusive access to "*My Coaching, Mentoring & Leadership Advisor*" GPT, a cutting-edge tool developed using OpenAI's ChatGPT technology. This custom GPT model is specifically designed to offer targeted assistance in leadership, coaching, and mentoring, enhancing your professional journey with AI-driven insights. To maximize its impact, we recommend using this GPT in conjunction with the prompts provided in this book. This synergistic approach will amplify your learning experience, offering a unique blend of expert guidance and personalized AI assistance. To access this GPT, please refer to the following chapter in this book.

2. **Prompt engineering for optimal outcomes:** We advocate for an informed, strategic approach to using the prompts provided in this book. Each prompt is meticulously engineered to serve a specific purpose and is accompanied by its intended goal, a guiding formula, and two illustrative examples. Text highlighted in **bold** and terms enclosed in square brackets **[ ]** are particularly conducive to customization. We encourage you to not just copy these prompts verbatim but to understand their underlying structure and adapt them to your unique circumstances. The more tailored the prompt, the more relevant and actionable the output will be.

3. **Differentiating complexities for broader utility:** The aim is to offer a broader perspective on how these prompts can be employed and customized. By engaging with a diverse array of prompts, you can develop a nuanced understanding of their underlying mechanisms, thereby gaining the flexibility to tailor them to multiple contexts or objectives.

4. **Integrative strategies for customization:** As you move through this book, you are encouraged to blend different strategies and tools to create customized plans. A well-crafted prompt elicits a higher-quality response; thus, investment in tailoring your inquiries is more than just a recommendation—it's a necessity for meaningful engagement with the book's content.

5. **Ethical considerations and critical thinking:** AI provides valuable insights, but it's crucial to critically evaluate this information. Use Chatbots' advice as a starting point for your strategies, complementing it with further research and ethical considerations. It's essential to remember that while AI can augment decision-making, it can't replace human wisdom.

6. **Communication excellence:** When crafting prompts for Chatbots, aim for clarity and precision. Open-ended questions often lead to more in-depth responses. For a tailored experience, you can also specify the persona or role you want the AI to assume, thereby aligning its feedback with your specific leadership or coaching context.

7. **Target audience, industry, and specificity:** Clearly defining your target audience and industry will enable you to fine-tune the strategies and insights you derive from this book and the accompanying AI resources. Whether you are a leadership consultant, executive coach, or HR professional, audience specificity enhances the utility of the guidance offered.

8. **Getting started with Chatbots:** For those new to the Chatbots platform, we provide a step-by-step guide to get you up and running, empowering you to leverage AI capabilities for your professional development in leadership and coaching.

Here is an overview of the appendices and how they can be integrated into your prompting:

- **Appendix No. 4** - Professions in Mentoring, Coaching, and Leadership: This appendix enumerates key professions that support personal and organizational development through guidance, training, and inspiration. Select the profession most relevant to your current challenge or opportunity to tailor your prompts, ensuring the most pertinent input from the Chatbot.

- **Appendix No. 5** - Specializations in Mentoring, Coaching, and Leadership: This section presents specialized roles within these fields, emphasizing excellence, innovation, and resilience in professional settings. Choose a specialization closely aligned with your specific challenge or opportunity to create effective prompts and receive the most relevant input from the Chatbot.
- **Appendix No. 6** - Tones for Responses from Chatbots: This appendix explores various writing tones you may want Chatbots to use in their responses to your prompts, ensuring alignment with your communication preferences.
- **Appendix No. 7** - Writing Styles for Responses from Chatbots: This section explores a variety of writing styles designed to enhance the clarity and effectiveness of the responses you seek to obtain from Chatbots, ensuring tailored and impactful communication.
- **Appendix No. 8** - Tagging System for Prompt Navigation: This appendix extends beyond the table of contents by offering three tags for each prompt in the book. These tags are carefully selected to assist readers in easily finding the most relevant prompts for their specific challenges or opportunities, ensuring a targeted and efficient use of the book's resources.

By strategically integrating AI tools and best practices, you can enhance not just your personal growth, but also the development of those you coach, mentor, and lead.

MEET "*MY COACHING, MENTORING & LEADERSHIP ADVISOR*" GPT

My Coaching, Mentoring & Leadership Advisor GPT, developed with OpenAI's ChatGPT technology, enhances your interaction with ChatGPT, offering a more tailored and responsive experience.

This custom GPT (Generative Pre-trained Transformer) model is expertly crafted to provide targeted help in leadership, coaching, and mentoring.

As a dynamic Artificial Intelligence companion, it aligns with your unique professional style and needs, providing tailored advice and insights to help navigate your leadership path.

Engaging with this GPT is incredibly intuitive, and simpler than you might expect. Once you access to ChatGPT, you'll be greeted by a user-friendly interface where you can input your questions or prompts.

The GPT responds almost instantly, offering valuable insights and guidance.

Whether you aim to enhance your leadership abilities, improve team dynamics, or foster personal and professional growth, *My Coaching, Mentoring & Leadership Advisor GPT* stands as your gateway to innovative professional development.

Accompanying this section is a screenshot showcasing the user interface you'll encounter when accessing 'My Coaching, Mentoring & Leadership Advisor' GPT. This visual reference provides a clear preview of what to expect, guiding you through your first steps in utilizing this innovative tool.

To start your journey towards advanced leadership and coaching skills, and to experience this unique blend of knowledge and technology, please scan this QR code.

Disclaimer: There's a monthly fee for using OpenAI's Plus plan, which you need to access the GPT I created for this book. Wanted to be clear – I don't get any income from OpenAI for suggesting their service. It's all about giving you great tools, and that's why I produced this GPT specifically for the book and for you. As of now, us GPT builders don't get a share of OpenAI's earnings, but if that ever changes – I'll update the disclaimer right away. Mauricio

FREE GOODWILL

Would you consider investing a minute to leave a lasting impression on someone's professional journey? Your experience and insights matter.

Right now, there's a professional, a mentor, or a leader seeking to elevate their capabilities. They're navigating the challenges of leadership, coaching, and perhaps even career transition. Your review could be a pivotal guide for them.

Think of reviews as more than just responses—they're endorsements, collective knowledge, and indicators of reliability. If this book offers you actionable insights or innovative strategies, could you share those experiences through a quick review? By doing so, you contribute to:

- Directing someone to tools and strategies that can heighten their leadership skills.
- Facilitating an individual's capacity to better mentor and coach.
- Enriching someone's perspective, which they might have otherwise overlooked.
- Catalyzing transformation in another's professional path.

By reviewing this book, you contribute to broadening the horizon of effective leadership, mentorship, and coaching for someone else. If you find value in this book, don't hesitate to share it within your network. People remember fondly those who introduced them to beneficial resources.

Enjoyed our book? Scan the QR code to quickly leave a review. Your feedback is invaluable!

Your engagement is much appreciated. Thank you for becoming an advocate for impactful leadership and personal development.

Best regards,

Mauricio

Scan the QR code to access our book collection.

TABLE OF CONTENTS

ACCOUNTABILITY

PROMPT No 1

Engagement - Virtual Environment - Team Presence

To acquire strategies for promoting and ensuring the full presence and engagement of a team member with their colleagues.

In the context of a **virtual working environment**, as a **Professional Coach** and in an **empathetic and understanding tone**, could you explain the steps **I** should take to ensure **the full presence** of a **colleague** with their **colleagues**?

In the context of **[contextual challenge/opportunity]**, as a **[profession]** and in a **[tone of voice]**, could you explain the steps **[I/Name/Role]** should take to ensure the **[desired outcome]** of a **[colleague/employee/team member]** with their **[colleagues/team/client]**

Example 1: In the context of a remote working environment, as a Professional Coach and in an empathetic tone, could you explain the steps a team leader should take to ensure the full presence of a team member with their colleagues?

Example 2: In the context of their onboarding process, as a Leadership Consultant and in a constructive tone, could you explain the steps a manager should take to ensure the full engagement of a new hire with their team?

PROMPT No 2

Courage Enhancement - Risk-Taking - Innovative Culture

To gain insights on specific ways to provide a team with the necessary tools, resources, and support to enhance their courage and enable them to take more risks and make bolder decisions, fostering a culture of innovation and growth.

Given the goal of **enhancing courage and risk-taking in decision-making**, as a **Leadership Development Facilitator** and in an **empowering and motivational tone**, could you suggest specific ways I can provide my **team** with the necessary tools, resources, and support?

20

Given the goal of **[contextual challenge/opportunity]**, as a **[profession]** and in a **[tone of voice]**, could you suggest specific ways **[I/Name/Role]** can provide **[my/their]** **[team/group/department]** with the necessary tools, resources, and support?

Example 1: Given the goal of enhancing courage and risk-taking in decision-making in a startup environment, as a Business Coach and in an energetic and inspiring tone, could you suggest specific ways a startup founder can provide their team with the necessary tools, resources, and support?

Example 2: As a Performance Coach, in an enthusiastic and motivating tone, could you suggest specific ways I can provide my research and development team with the necessary tools, resources, and support? This advice is particularly relevant given the goal of enhancing courage and risk-taking in decision-making in a competitive tech industry.

ACTION

PROMPT No 3

Strategic Planning - Competitive Advantage - Team Performance

To gain a comprehensive and detailed strategic plan that can be implemented by the team to successfully achieve their objectives or gain a significant competitive advantage, with the aim of enhancing team performance and competitiveness.

As a **Management Consultant**, adopting a **clear and concise tone**, could you please provide a comprehensive and detailed strategic plan that can be implemented by **my team** to **successfully achieve their objectives or gain a significant competitive advantage**? Your response should include a thorough outline of the steps, strategies, and tactics that need to be taken into consideration. This is particularly relevant given the goal of **enhancing team performance and competitiveness**.

As a **[profession]**, adopting a **[tone of voice]**, could you please provide a comprehensive and detailed strategic plan that can be implemented by **[my/their] [team/group/department]** to **[contextual challenge/opportunity]**? Your response should include a thorough outline of the steps, strategies, and tactics that need to be taken into consideration. This is particularly relevant given the goal of **[desired outcome]**.

Example 1: As a Leadership Development Consultant, adopting an encouraging and solution-oriented tone, could you please provide a comprehensive and detailed strategic plan that can be implemented by the marketing department to successfully achieve their objectives or gain a significant competitive advantage? Your response should include a thorough outline of the steps, strategies, and tactics that need to be taken into consideration. This is particularly relevant given the goal of enhancing department performance and competitiveness.

Example 2: Adopting an optimistic and motivating tone, as a Business Coach, could you please provide a comprehensive and detailed strategic plan that can be implemented by my project team to successfully achieve their objectives or gain a significant competitive advantage? Your response should include a thorough outline of the steps, strategies, and tactics that need to be taken into consideration. This is particularly relevant given the goal of enhancing team performance and competitiveness within the project.

PROMPT No 4

Self-Discovery - Personal Development - Strengths

To gain a comprehensive and detailed step-by-step process that can be followed to effectively engage in self-discovery, enabling the identification and understanding of personal strengths and weaknesses.

As a **Personal Development Coach**, adopting an **encouraging and supportive tone**, could you provide a **precise and comprehensive step-by-step process** that I can adopt to **thoroughly and successfully engage in self-discovery**? This is particularly relevant given the goal of **identifying and understanding my individual strengths and weaknesses**.

As a [profession], adopting a [tone of voice], could you provide a [description of process] that [I/Name/Role] can adopt to [contextual challenge/opportunity]? This is particularly relevant given the goal of [desired outcome].

Example 1: As a Life Coach, adopting a compassionate and patient tone, could you provide a precise and comprehensive step-by-step process that a new entrepreneur can adopt to thoroughly and successfully engage in self-discovery? This is particularly relevant given the goal of identifying and understanding their individual strengths and weaknesses as they start their business journey.

Example 2: As a Career Counselor, adopting a professional and empathetic tone, could you provide a precise and comprehensive step-by-step process that a recent graduate can adopt to thoroughly and successfully engage in self-discovery? This is particularly relevant given the goal of identifying and understanding their individual strengths and weaknesses as they navigate the job market.

Decision-Making - Bold Choices - Informed Analysis

Goal

To gain insights on the specific factors that should be thoroughly analyzed and considered when making a bold decision that will affect a team, ensuring informed and effective decision-making.

Prompt

As a **Decision-Making Expert**, adopting a **clear and concise tone**, could you guide **me** on the specific factors that **I** should thoroughly analyze and consider when making a bold decision that will affect **my team**? This is particularly relevant given the goal of **ensuring informed and effective decision-making**.

Formula

As a **[profession]**, adopting a **[tone of voice]**, could you guide **[me/Name/Role]** on the specific factors that **[I/Name/Role]** should thoroughly analyze and consider when making a bold decision that will affect **[my/their]** **[team/group/department]**? This is particularly relevant given the goal of **[desired outcome]**.

Examples

Example 1: As a Business Strategist, adopting a straightforward and analytical tone, could you guide a project manager on the specific factors that they should thoroughly analyze and consider when making a bold decision that will affect their project team? This is particularly relevant given the goal of ensuring informed and effective decision-making.

Example 2: As a Leadership Consultant, adopting a supportive and professional tone, could you guide me on the specific factors that I should thoroughly analyze and consider when making a bold decision that will affect my sales team? This is particularly relevant given the goal of ensuring informed and effective decision-making.

AWARENESS

PROMPT No 6

Tags

Emotional Intelligence - Fear Addressing - Team Morale

Goal

To gain specific strategies or methods to uncover the hidden fears or anxieties that team members may have regarding their work, fostering an understanding of these fears and how to address them to enhance team morale and productivity.

Prompt

As an **Emotional Intelligence Coach**, adopting a **patient and empathetic tone**, could you suggest specific strategies or methods that **I** can employ to uncover **the hidden fears or anxieties** that **my team members** may have regarding their work? This is particularly relevant given the goal of **understanding and addressing these hidden fears to enhance team morale and productivity**.

Formula

As a **[profession]**, adopting a **[tone of voice]**, could you suggest specific strategies or methods that [I/Name/Role] can employ to uncover the **[contextual challenge/opportunity]** that **[my/their]** **[team/group/department]** may have regarding their work? This is particularly relevant given the goal of **[desired outcome]**.

Example 1: Adopting a respectful and considerate tone, as a Leadership Development Consultant, could you suggest specific strategies or methods that a department head can employ to uncover the hidden fears or anxieties that their faculty may have regarding academic work? This is particularly relevant given the goal of understanding and addressing these hidden fears to enhance academic morale and productivity.

Example 2: As a Team Coach, adopting an understanding and supportive tone, could you suggest specific strategies or methods that I can employ to uncover the hidden fears or anxieties that my project team may have regarding project work? This is particularly relevant given the goal of understanding and addressing these hidden fears to enhance project morale and productivity.

PROMPT No 7

Personal Growth - Achievement Strategies - Individual Development

To gain specific strategies or methods that can be employed to effectively explore and enhance the personal growth and development of each individual team member, particularly in relation to their accomplishments or setbacks in achieving their goals. This is aimed at fostering personal development and goal achievement within the team.

As a **Leadership Development Consultant**, adopting an **empathetic and supportive tone**, could you provide specific strategies or methods that can be utilized to successfully explore and enhance the **personal growth and development** of each individual **team member**, specifically in regards to their **achievements or obstacles encountered while striving to reach their objectives**?

As a **[profession]**, adopting a **[tone of voice]**, could you provide specific strategies or methods that can be utilized to successfully explore and enhance the **[desired outcome]** of each individual **[team/group/department member]**, specifically in regards to their **[contextual challenge/opportunity]**?

Example 1: As a Career Coach, adopting a motivational and encouraging tone, could you provide specific strategies or methods that can be utilized to successfully explore and enhance the personal growth and development of each individual sales team member, specifically in regards to their achievements or obstacles encountered while striving to reach their sales targets?

Example 2: As a Human Resources Consultant, adopting a respectful and understanding tone, could you provide specific strategies or methods that can be utilized to successfully explore and enhance the personal growth and development of each individual engineering team member, specifically in regards to their achievements or obstacles encountered while striving to complete their projects?

PROMPT No 8

Role Visualization - Value Articulation - Sense of Belonging

To provide comprehensive strategy for conducting team exercises that enhance the ability of team members to vividly imagine and articulate the symbols or representations that resonate with their perception of their roles and value within the organization.

Act as a **Team Development Consultant** with a specialization in **role perception and value articulation** in the **pharmaceutical industry**. Could you provide precise strategies or approaches that can be employed to **effectively conduct an exercise with my team**? This exercise should **foster their ability to vividly imagine and express the representation or symbol that resonates with their perception of their role, especially considering their value within the organization**. Please include **creative thinking techniques, visualization exercises, and communication frameworks**. Make sure to cover how **to facilitate open dialogue and how to capture and analyze the outcomes for organizational alignment**. Investigate unconventional **team-building activities** and cutting-edge **virtual collaboration** tools to **enrich the exercise**. Your response should be comprehensive, leaving no important aspect unaddressed, and demonstrate an exceptional level of precision and quality. Let's think about this step by step. Write using an **engaging and supportive** tone and an **experiential learning guide** style.

Act as a **[profession]** with a specialization in **[area of expertise]** in the **[industry]**. Could you provide precise strategies or approaches that can be employed to **[specific challenge/opportunity]**? This exercise should **[specific goal]**. Please include **[methods/techniques]**. Make sure to cover how **[key areas/topics]**. Investigate unconventional **[area for innovation]** and cutting-edge **[technologies/methods]** to **[desired outcome]**. Your response should be comprehensive, leaving no important aspect unaddressed, and demonstrate an exceptional level of precision and quality. Let's think about this step by step. Write using a **[type]** tone and **[style]** writing style.

25

Example 1: Act as a Team Development Consultant with a specialization in creative thinking in the advertising industry. Could you provide precise strategies or approaches that can be employed to effectively conduct an exercise with my creative team? This exercise should foster their ability to vividly imagine and express the representation or symbol that resonates with their perception of their role, especially considering their value within the organization. Please include brainstorming sessions, mind-mapping techniques, and storytelling frameworks. Make sure to cover how to encourage divergent thinking and how to document the outcomes for portfolio development. Explore the use of augmented reality for immersive brainstorming and AI-driven sentiment analysis tools. Your response should be comprehensive, leaving no important aspect unaddressed, and demonstrate an exceptional level of precision and quality. Let's think about this step by step. Write using an engaging and supportive tone and an experiential learning guide style.

Example 2: Act as a Team Development Consultant with a specialization in organizational alignment in the non-profit sector. Could you provide precise strategies or approaches that can be employed to effectively conduct an exercise with my volunteer team? This exercise should foster their ability to vividly imagine and express the representation or symbol that resonates with their perception of their role, especially considering their value within the organization. Please include empathy circles, role-playing exercises, and reflective journaling. Make sure to cover how to facilitate emotional intelligence and how to align the outcomes with organizational mission and values. Delve into the use of virtual reality for empathy training and blockchain for transparent value alignment. Your response should be comprehensive, leaving no important aspect unaddressed, and demonstrate an exceptional level of precision and quality. Let's think about this step by step. Write using an engaging and supportive tone and an experiential learning guide style.

PROMPT No. 9

Tags
Thought Awareness - Responsibility Management - Interaction Impact

Goal
To gain specific strategies or techniques that can be used to consistently and effectively maintain awareness of how one's thoughts impact their responsibilities and interactions with team members.

Prompt
As a **Leadership Development Consultant**, adopting a **reflective and insightful tone**, could you provide specific strategies or techniques that can be used to consistently and effectively maintain awareness of how one's thoughts impact their responsibilities and interactions with team members? This is particularly relevant given the goal of fostering self-awareness and effective team collaboration.

Formula
As a **[profession]**, adopting a **[tone of voice]**, could you provide specific strategies or techniques that can be used to **[contextual challenge/opportunity]** of how **[one's/my/their]** thoughts impact **[their/my/one's]** responsibilities and interactions with **[team members/colleagues/group]**? This is particularly relevant given the goal of **[desired outcome]**.

Examples
Example 1: As a Team Coach, adopting a reflective and insightful tone, could you provide specific strategies or techniques that can be used to consistently and effectively maintain awareness of how a project manager's thoughts impact their responsibilities and interactions

with project team members? This is particularly relevant given the goal of fostering self-awareness and effective project team collaboration.

Example 2: As a Human Resources Consultant, adopting a reflective and insightful tone, could you provide specific strategies or techniques that can be used to consistently and effectively maintain awareness of how an HR manager's thoughts impact their responsibilities and interactions with HR team members? This is particularly relevant given the goal of fostering self-awareness and effective HR team collaboration.

PROMPT No 10

Tags

Recognition - Beliefs - Management

Goal

To gain detailed methods and approaches to effectively enhance the recognition and understanding of the underlying beliefs or assumptions that guide the operations of a team, as well as the potential outcomes or impacts that arise from these beliefs or assumptions, fostering an enhancement in team understanding and management of underlying beliefs and assumptions.

Prompt

As an **Organizational Development Consultant**, adopting a **clear and concise tone**, could you explain in detail the specific methods and approaches that **I** can implement to effectively enhance the recognition and understanding of **the underlying beliefs or assumptions** that guide the operations of **my team**, as well as the potential outcomes or impacts that arise from these **beliefs or assumptions**? This is particularly relevant given the goal of enhancing team understanding and management of underlying beliefs and assumptions.

Formula

As a **[profession]**, adopting a **[tone of voice]**, could you explain in detail the specific methods and approaches that **[I/Name/Role]** can implement to effectively enhance the recognition and understanding of **[contextual challenge/opportunity]** that guide the operations of **[my/their] [team/group/department]**, as well as the potential outcomes or impacts that arise from these? This is particularly relevant given the goal of **[desired outcome]**.

Examples

Example 1: Adopting a professional and respectful tone, as a Management Consultant, could you explain in detail the specific methods and approaches that a department head can implement to effectively enhance the recognition and understanding of the underlying beliefs or assumptions that guide the operations of their faculty, as well as the potential outcomes or impacts that arise from these beliefs or assumptions? This is particularly relevant given the goal of enhancing faculty understanding and management of underlying beliefs and assumptions.

Example 2: As a Leadership Development Facilitator, adopting a supportive and solution-oriented tone, could you explain in detail the specific methods and approaches that I can implement to effectively enhance the recognition and understanding of the underlying beliefs or assumptions that guide the operations of my project team, as well as the potential outcomes or impacts that arise from these beliefs or assumptions? This is particularly relevant given the goal of enhancing project team understanding and management of underlying beliefs and assumptions.

PROMPT No 11

Empathy - Emotion - Interpretation

To gain guidance on how to effectively interpret the cues and signals exhibited by team members in order to gain a deeper understanding of their emotions and feelings, fostering an enhancement in emotional intelligence and empathy within the team.

As an **Emotional Intelligence Coach**, adopting a **patient and empathetic tone**, could you guide **me** on how **I** can effectively interpret the cues and signals exhibited by **my team** members in order to gain a deeper understanding of **their emotions and feelings**? This is particularly relevant given the goal of **enhancing emotional intelligence and empathy within the team**.

As a **[profession]**, adopting a **[tone of voice]**, could you guide **[me/Name/Role]** on how **[I/they]** can effectively interpret the cues and signals exhibited by **[my/their]** **[team/group/department]** members in order to gain a deeper understanding of **[contextual challenge/opportunity]**? This is particularly relevant given the goal of **[desired outcome]**.

Example 1: Adopting a respectful and considerate tone, as a Leadership Coach, could you guide a department head on how they can effectively interpret the cues and signals exhibited by their faculty members in order to gain a deeper understanding of their emotions and feelings? This is particularly relevant given the goal of enhancing emotional intelligence and empathy within the faculty.

Example 2: As a Human Resources Consultant, adopting a supportive and understanding tone, could you guide me on how I can effectively interpret the cues and signals exhibited by my project team members in order to gain a deeper understanding of their emotions and feelings? This is particularly relevant given the goal of enhancing emotional intelligence and empathy within the project team.

BELIEF

PROMPT No 12

Counter-evidence - Critical-Thinking -Evaluation

To obtain comprehensive and high-quality suggestions on specific methods or techniques that can effectively foster critical thinking and encourage the consideration of counter-evidence among team members or oneself when evaluating a business plan or strategy.

As a **Business Strategy Consultant**, adopting an **informative and insightful tone**, could you provide detailed suggestions on specific methods or techniques that can effectively foster **critical thinking and encourage the consideration of counter-evidence** among **my team members** when **evaluating a business plan or strategy**?

As a **[profession]**, adopting a **[tone of voice]**, could you provide detailed suggestions on specific methods or techniques that can effectively foster **[desired outcome]** among **[my/their]** **[team/group/department]** when **[contextual challenge/opportunity]**?

Example 1: As a Leadership Development Consultant, adopting an encouraging and supportive tone, could you provide detailed suggestions on specific methods or techniques that can effectively foster critical thinking and encourage the consideration of counter-evidence among faculty when evaluating a new academic program or curriculum?

Example 2: As a Project Management Consultant, adopting a clear and concise tone, could you provide detailed suggestions on specific methods or techniques that can effectively foster critical thinking and encourage the consideration of counter-evidence among my project team when evaluating a project plan or strategy?

PROMPT No 13

Assumptions - Conflict - Resolution

To gain a comprehensive understanding of the underlying assumptions that the team is making while addressing a specific issue, thereby enabling a more effective and informed approach to problem-solving.

As a **Team Development Consultant**, adopting a **detailed and analytical tone**, could you help **me** identify and provide detailed explanations of the various assumptions **my team** is making when addressing **a conflict with their suppliers**? By doing so, we aim to gain a thorough understanding of the underlying beliefs and premises that underpin their approach to this **conflict**.

As a **[profession]**, adopting a **[tone of voice]**, could you help **[me/Name/Role]** identify and provide detailed explanations of the various assumptions **[my/their]** **[team/group/department]** is making when addressing a **[contextual challenge/opportunity]**? By doing so, we aim to gain a thorough understanding of the underlying beliefs and premises that underpin our approach to this **[contextual challenge/opportunity]**.

Example 1: As a Business Coach, adopting a detailed and analytical tone, could you help the project manager identify and provide detailed explanations of the various assumptions their project team is making when addressing a project delay? By doing so, we aim to gain a thorough understanding of the underlying beliefs and premises that underpin their approach to this project delay.

Example 2: As a Leadership Consultant, adopting a detailed and analytical tone, could you help me identify and provide detailed explanations of the various assumptions my sales team is making when addressing a decline in sales? By doing so, we aim to gain a thorough understanding of the underlying beliefs and premises that underpin our approach to this decline in sales.

PROMPT No 14

Contradiction - Values - Resolution

To gain insights on how to handle a workplace situation that directly contradicts personal beliefs or values, ensuring the response is comprehensive, precise, and of high quality.

As a **HR Professional**, adopting a **thoughtful and empathetic tone**, could you explain in great detail the specific steps I should take to navigate and resolve a workplace scenario that **directly contradicts my personal beliefs or values**? This is particularly relevant given the goal of **understanding how to handle situations that conflict with personal values in the workplace**.

As a **[profession]**, adopting a **[tone of voice]**, could you explain in great detail the specific steps that **[I/Name/Role]** can take to navigate and resolve a workplace scenario that **[contextual challenge/opportunity]**? This is particularly relevant given the goal of **[desired outcome]**.

Example 1: As a seasoned HR Professional, adopting a compassionate and understanding tone, could you explain in great detail the specific steps that a department head can take to navigate and resolve a workplace scenario that directly contradicts their team's personal beliefs or values? This is particularly relevant given the goal of understanding how to handle situations that conflict with personal values in the workplace.

Example 2: As an experienced HR consultant, adopting a considerate and empathetic tone, could you explain in great detail the specific steps that a team leader can take to navigate and resolve a workplace scenario that directly contradicts their personal beliefs or values? This is particularly relevant given the goal of understanding how to handle situations that conflict with personal values in the workplace.

PROMPT No 15

Satisfaction - Fulfillment - Communication

To identify and communicate specific beliefs or assumptions that will contribute to the overall job satisfaction and personal fulfillment of a team.

As a **Team Leader**, adopting a **supportive and encouraging tone**, could you help **me** identify **specific beliefs or assumptions that I can effectively communicate to my team**? This is particularly relevant given the goal of **enhancing their overall job satisfaction and personal fulfillment**.

As a **[profession]**, adopting a **[tone of voice]**, could you help **[me/Name/Role]** identify **[contextual challenge/opportunity]**? This is particularly relevant given the goal of **[desired outcome]**.

Example 1: As a Human Resources Manager, adopting a compassionate and understanding tone, could you help me identify specific beliefs or assumptions that I can effectively communicate to my HR team? This is particularly relevant given the goal of enhancing their overall job satisfaction and personal fulfillment.

Example 2: As a Project Manager, adopting a motivational and inspiring tone, could you help me identify specific beliefs or assumptions that I can effectively communicate to my project team? This is particularly relevant given the goal of enhancing their overall job satisfaction and personal fulfillment.

PROMPT No 16

Tags

Transformation - Assumptions - Facilitation

Goal

To gain insights on how to effectively facilitate a shift in a team's underlying beliefs or assumptions.

Prompt

Given the challenge of **transforming deeply ingrained beliefs or assumptions**, could you, as an **Executive Coach** and in a **respectful and patient tone**, detail how I could facilitate this switch in **my team**'s underlying beliefs or assumptions?

Formula

Given the challenge of **[contextual challenge/opportunity]**, could you, as a **[profession]** and in a **[tone of voice]**, detail how **[I/Name/Role]** could facilitate this switch in **[my/their]** **[team/group/department]'s** underlying beliefs or assumptions?

Examples

Example 1: Given the challenge of transforming traditional work methods, could you, as a change management consultant and in a diplomatic and professional tone, detail how a manager could facilitate this switch in their team's underlying beliefs or assumptions?

Example 2: Could you, as a leadership development facilitator and in an open-minded and considerate tone, detail how I could facilitate a switch in my team's underlying assumptions about remote work, especially given the challenge of transitioning to a virtual work environment?

PROMPT No 17

Tags

Belief - Motivation - Action

Goal

To gain a detailed explanation of actionable steps that can be taken to instill a strong sense of belief within a team, fostering motivation for positive changes in career or performance by altering the decision-making process.

Prompt

As an **Executive Coach**, adopting an **inspiring and motivating tone**, could you provide a detailed explanation of actionable steps that can be taken to **instill a strong sense of belief** within **my team**? This is particularly relevant given the goal of **motivating them to make**

positive changes in their career or performance by altering their decision-making process.

As a **[profession]**, adopting a **[tone of voice]**, could you provide a detailed explanation of actionable steps that can be taken to **[desired outcome]** within **[my/their]** **[team/group/department]?** This is particularly relevant given the goal of **[contextual challenge/opportunity].**

Example 1: Adopting an encouraging and supportive tone, as a Leadership Development Consultant, could you provide a detailed explanation of actionable steps that can be taken to instill a strong sense of belief within a faculty? This is particularly relevant given the goal of motivating them to make positive changes in their academic performance by altering their decision-making process.

Example 2: As a Team Coach, adopting an enthusiastic and optimistic tone, could you provide a detailed explanation of actionable steps that can be taken to instill a strong sense of belief within my project team? This is particularly relevant given the goal of motivating them to make positive changes in their project performance by altering their decision-making process.

CHALLENGE

PROMPT No 18

Career - Assistance - Progression

To gain insights on identifying signs of a colleague's career going off-course and to learn actionable steps to assist them in getting back on track, fostering career progression and a supportive work environment.

As a **Career Coach**, adopting a **supportive and respectful tone**, could you help **me** identify signs that might indicate a **colleague's career is veering off-course**? Additionally, could you suggest actions I can take to assist them in getting back on the right track, especially considering the challenge of maintaining career progression?

As a **[profession]**, adopting a **[tone of voice]**, could you help **[me/Name/Role]** identify signs that might indicate a **[team member/colleague's]** **[contextual challenge/opportunity]?** Additionally, could you suggest actions **[I/Name/Role]** can take to assist them in **[desired outcome]**, especially considering **[contextual challenge/opportunity]?**

Example 1: Adopting a collaborative and professional tone, as a Leadership Development Consultant, could you help a department head identify signs that might indicate a faculty member's career is veering off-course? Especially considering the challenge of maintaining academic progression, could you suggest actions they can take to assist them in getting back on the right track?

Example 2: As a Human Resources (HR) Consultant, with a clear and concise tone, could you help me identify signs that might indicate a team member's career is veering off-course in a high-stress environment? Additionally, considering the challenge of maintaining high performance, could you suggest actions I can take to assist them in getting back on the right track?

PROMPT No 19

Diversity - Problem-Solving - Strategies

To gain insights and strategies for facilitating diverse problem-solving perspectives within a team, enhancing the team's ability to approach and solve problems from various angles.

As a **Leadership Coach**, adopting a **collaborative and open-minded tone**, could you provide **me** with strategies and techniques to explore with **my team** different ways t**o look at a problem**? This is particularly relevant given the goal of **fostering a diverse problem-solving culture within the team**.

As a **[profession]**, adopting a **[tone of voice]**, could you provide **[me/Name/Role]** with strategies and techniques to explore with **[my/their] [team/group/department]** different ways to **[contextual challenge/opportunity]**? This is particularly relevant given the goal of **[desired outcome]**.

Example 1: As a Team Development Specialist, adopting a supportive and encouraging tone, could you provide me with strategies and techniques to explore with my project team different ways to look at a project delay? This is particularly relevant given the goal of fostering a diverse problem-solving culture within the project team.
Example 2: As a Business Mentor, adopting a constructive and professional tone, could you provide me with strategies and techniques to explore with my logistic team different ways to look at a delivery shortfall? This is particularly relevant given the goal of fostering a diverse problem-solving culture within the logistic team.

PROMPT No 20

Resilience - Problem-Solving - Empowerment

To gain specific strategies or methods for promoting resilience and problem-solving abilities within a team, empowering them to effectively tackle various challenges.

As a **Leadership Development Consultant**, adopting a solution-oriented and supportive tone, could you recommend specific strategies or methods that **I** can implement to **promote resilience and problem-solving abilities** within **my team**? I am seeking comprehensive and precise suggestions that will empower them to effectively tackle the various challenges they may face.

As a **[profession]**, adopting a **[tone of voice]**, could you recommend specific strategies or methods that **[I/Name/Role]** can implement to **[desired outcome]** within **[my/their]** **[team/group/department]**? I am seeking comprehensive and precise suggestions that will empower them to **[contextual challenge/opportunity]**.

Example 1: As a Team Coach, adopting a motivational and encouraging tone, could you recommend specific strategies or methods that a maintenance department head can implement to promote resilience and problem-solving abilities within their maintenance team? They are seeking comprehensive and precise suggestions that will empower the faculty to effectively tackle the various academic challenges they may face.

Example 2: As a Business Mentor, adopting a constructive and supportive tone, could you recommend specific strategies or methods that I can implement to promote resilience and problem-solving abilities within my sales team? I am seeking comprehensive and precise suggestions that will empower them to effectively tackle the various sales challenges they may face.

PROMPT No 21

Learning - Mistakes - Growth

To gain insights and strategies on how to develop a mindset that perceives mistakes as valuable opportunities for learning, rather than as failures, fostering a growth mindset and a culture of continuous learning.

As a **Personal Development Coach**, adopting an **encouraging and supportive tone**, could you provide detailed insights and strategies on how I can help **my team** develop a mindset that perceives **mistakes** as valuable opportunities for learning, rather than as failures? This is particularly relevant given the goal of **fostering a growth mindset and a culture of continuous learning within the team**.

As a **[profession]**, adopting a **[tone of voice]**, could you provide detailed insights and strategies on how **[I/Name/Role]** can help **[my/their]** **[team/group/department]** develop a mindset that perceives **[contextual challenge/opportunity]** as valuable opportunities for learning, rather than as failures? This is particularly relevant given the goal of **[desired outcome]**.

Example 1: As a Leadership Development Consultant, adopting a motivational and positive tone, could you provide detailed insights and strategies on how a department head can help their IT team develop a mindset that perceives technical challenges as valuable opportunities for learning, rather than as failures? This is particularly relevant given the goal of fostering a growth mindset and a culture of continuous learning within the IT team.

Example 2: As a Team Coach, adopting an empathetic and understanding tone, could you provide detailed insights and strategies on how I can help my project team develop a mindset that perceives project setbacks as valuable opportunities for learning, rather than as failures? This is particularly relevant given the goal of fostering a growth mindset and a culture of continuous learning within the project team.

PROMPT No 22

Communication - HR - Obstacle-Resolution

To gain specific strategies and techniques to enhance communication within a team and effectively address and overcome obstacles encountered in their work.

As a **Human Resources (HR) Consultant**, utilizing a **clear and concise tone**, could you provide strategies and techniques to **enhance communication** within the **HR team** and **address obstacles** encountered during **recruitment efforts**?

As a **[profession]**, utilizing a **[tone of voice]**, could you provide strategies and techniques to **[desired outcome]** within **[my/their] [team/group/department]** and **[desired outcome]** encountered during **[contextual challenge/opportunity]**?

Example 1: As a Project Manager, utilizing a clear and concise tone, could you provide strategies and techniques to enhance communication within my project team and address obstacles encountered during our software development project?

Example 2: As a Sales Manager, utilizing a motivational and enthusiastic tone, could you provide strategies and techniques to enhance communication within the sales team and address obstacles encountered during our quarterly sales drive?

CHANGE

PROMPT No 23

Relationship-Building - Collaboration - Work-Environment

To gain a detailed plan of action to enhance the working relationships of a team with their colleagues and clients, fostering a positive and productive work environment.

As a **Business Coach**, adopting a **collaborative and respectful tone**, could you provide a detailed plan of action that I can implement to **enhance the working relationships** of **my team** with their colleagues and clients? This is particularly relevant given the goal of **fostering a positive and productive work environment**.

As a **[profession]**, adopting a **[tone of voice]**, could you provide a detailed plan of action that **[I/Name/Role]** can implement to **[desired outcome]** of **[my/their] [team/group/department]** with their colleagues and clients? This is particularly relevant given the goal of **[desired outcome]**.

Example 1: Adopting a supportive and professional tone, as a Leadership Development Consultant, could you provide a detailed plan of action that a department head can implement to enhance the working relationships of their faculty with their colleagues and students? This is particularly relevant given the goal of fostering a positive and productive academic environment.

Example 2: As a Team Coach, adopting a clear and concise tone, could you provide a detailed plan of action that I can implement to enhance the working relationships of my project team with their colleagues and stakeholders? This is particularly relevant given the goal of fostering a positive and productive project environment.

PROMPT No 24

Tags
Future-Readiness - Leadership - Perspective-Shift

Goal
To acquire specific knowledge or skills at present that will enable the effective recognition and guidance of necessary changes in a team's perspectives in the future.

Prompt
As a **Leadership Development Consultant**, adopting an **educational and forward-thinking tone**, could you suggest what specific knowledge or skills I should acquire at present in order to effectively recognize and guide **my team** towards the necessary changes in their perspectives in the future?

Formula
As a **[profession]**, adopting a **[tone of voice]**, could you suggest what specific knowledge or skills **[I/Name/Role]** should acquire at present in order to effectively recognize and guide **[my/their] [team/group/department]** towards the necessary changes in their perspectives in the future?

Examples
Example 1: As a Team Coach, adopting a supportive and insightful tone, could you suggest what specific knowledge or skills a department head should acquire at present in order to effectively recognize and guide their faculty towards the necessary changes in their perspectives in the future? **Example 2:** As a Business Coach, adopting a motivational and strategic tone, could you suggest what specific knowledge or skills I should acquire at present in order to effectively recognize and guide my project team towards the necessary changes in their perspectives in the future?

PROMPT No 25

Tags
Evaluation - Consequence - Work-Methods

Goal
To gain specific techniques or approaches that can be employed to conduct a comprehensive evaluation of the impacts on a team's work if they decide to continue with their existing work methods and routines, fostering an understanding of the consequences of maintaining current work practices.

Prompt

As an **Organizational Development Consultant**, adopting an **analytical and strategic tone**, could you suggest specific techniques or approaches that I can employ to conduct a comprehensive evaluation of the impacts on **my team's** work if they decide to **continue with their existing work methods and routines**? This is particularly relevant given the goal of understanding the consequences of **maintaining current work practices**.

As a **[profession]**, adopting a **[tone of voice]**, could you suggest specific techniques or approaches that **[I/Name/Role]** can employ to conduct a comprehensive evaluation of the impacts on **[my/their] [team/group/department]**'s work if they decide to **[contextual challenge/opportunity]**? This is particularly relevant given the goal of **[desired outcome]**.

Example 1: As a Business Analyst, adopting a data-driven and systematic tone, could you suggest specific techniques or approaches that a project manager can employ to conduct a comprehensive evaluation of the impacts on their project team's work if they decide to continue with their existing work methods and routines? This is particularly relevant given the goal of understanding the consequences of maintaining current project management practices.

Example 2: As a Management Consultant, adopting a logical and insightful tone, could you suggest specific techniques or approaches that I can employ to conduct a comprehensive evaluation of the impacts on my sales team's work if they decide to continue with their existing sales methods and routines? This is particularly relevant given the goal of understanding the consequences of maintaining current sales practices.

COMMITMENT

PROMPT No 26

Motivation - Ownership - Vision

To gain specific and detailed strategies or approaches to successfully motivate and inspire a team to take full ownership of their responsibilities and actively work towards accomplishing a common vision, fostering a sense of ownership and shared vision within the team.

As a **Leadership Development Facilitator**, adopting an **inspirational and motivating tone**, could you provide specific and detailed strategies or approaches that I can implement to successfully motivate and inspire **my team** to take full ownership of their responsibilities and actively work towards accomplishing **our common vision**? This is particularly relevant given the goal of **fostering a sense of ownership and shared vision within the team**.

As a **[profession]**, adopting a **[tone of voice]**, could you provide specific and detailed strategies or approaches that **[I/Name/Role]** can implement to successfully motivate and inspire **[my/their] [team/group/department]** to take full ownership of their responsibilities and actively work towards accomplishing **[contextual challenge/opportunity]**? This is particularly relevant given the goal of **[desired outcome]**.

Example 1: Adopting an encouraging and supportive tone, as a Talent Development Specialist, could you provide specific and detailed strategies or approaches that a department head can implement to successfully motivate and inspire their faculty to take full ownership of their responsibilities and actively work towards accomplishing their common vision? This is particularly relevant given the goal of fostering a sense of ownership and shared vision within the faculty.

Example 2: As a Business Coach, adopting an optimistic and energetic tone, could you provide specific and detailed strategies or approaches that I can implement to successfully motivate and inspire my project team to take full ownership of their responsibilities and actively work towards accomplishing our common vision? This is particularly relevant given the goal of fostering a sense of ownership and shared vision within the project team.

PROMPT No 27

Tags
Dedication - Strategy - Goal-Progress

Goal
To gain specific strategies to effectively encourage and enhance a team's dedication and motivation in fulfilling their responsibilities and progressing towards their goals.

Prompt
As a **Leadership Development Consultant**, adopting a **motivational and encouraging tone**, could you provide specific strategies that I can implement to effectively encourage and enhance my **team's dedication and motivation** in fulfilling their responsibilities and progressing towards **our company's goals**?

Formula
As a **[profession]**, adopting a **[tone of voice]**, could you provide specific strategies that **[I/Name/Role]** can implement to effectively encourage and enhance **[my/their]** **[team/group/department]'s [desired outcome]** in fulfilling their responsibilities and progressing towards **[contextual challenge/opportunity]**?

Examples
Example 1: As a Team Coach, adopting an inspiring and supportive tone, could you provide specific strategies that a HR head can implement to effectively encourage and enhance their HR team's dedication and motivation in fulfilling their responsibilities and progressing towards their employee's engagement goals?   **Example 2:** As a Business Coach, adopting a positive and motivational tone, could you provide specific strategies that I can implement to effectively encourage and enhance my construction project team's dedication and motivation in fulfilling their responsibilities and progressing towards our construction completion goal?

CREATIVITY

PROMPT No 28

Tags
Self-Assessment - Evaluation - Improvement

Goal

To gain a detailed understanding of how to guide a team in conducting a comprehensive and insightful self-assessment process, including specific lines of questioning or areas of investigation to ensure a thorough evaluation.

As a **Leadership Development Consultant**, adopting a **supportive and instructive tone**, could you provide guidance on how I can effectively lead **my team** in conducting a comprehensive and insightful self-assessment process? Specifically, what lines of questioning or areas of investigation should I propose to ensure a thorough evaluation? This is particularly relevant given the goal of **fostering self-awareness and continuous improvement within the team**.

As a **[profession]**, adopting a **[tone of voice]**, could you provide guidance on how **[I/Name/Role]** can effectively lead **[my/their]** **[team/group/department]** in **[contextual challenge/opportunity]**? Specifically, what lines of questioning or areas of investigation should **[I/Name/Role]** propose to ensure a thorough evaluation? This is particularly relevant given the goal of **[desired outcome]**.

Example 1: As a Team Coach, adopting a respectful and patient tone, could you provide guidance on how a project manager can effectively lead their project team in conducting a comprehensive and insightful self-assessment process? Specifically, what lines of questioning or areas of investigation should the project manager propose to ensure a thorough evaluation? This is particularly relevant given the goal of fostering self-awareness and continuous improvement within the project team.

Example 2: As a Human Resources Consultant, adopting a clear and concise tone, could you provide guidance on how I can effectively lead my marketing team in conducting a comprehensive and insightful self-assessment process? Specifically, what lines of questioning or areas of investigation should I propose to ensure a thorough evaluation? This is particularly relevant given the goal of fostering self-awareness and continuous improvement within the marketing team.

PROMPT No 29

Creativity - Innovation - Strategy

To gain specific strategies, methods, or exercises to successfully cultivate and promote creativity within a team, ultimately leading to the generation of groundbreaking ideas and solutions, fostering a culture of innovation and creativity.

As an **Innovation Consultant**, adopting an **inspirational and motivating tone**, could you provide specific strategies, methods, or exercises that **I** can utilize to successfully cultivate and promote creativity **within my team**, ultimately leading to the generation of groundbreaking ideas and solutions? This is particularly relevant given the goal of **fostering a culture of innovation and creativity**.

As a **[profession]**, adopting a **[tone of voice]**, could you provide specific strategies, methods, or exercises that **[I/Name/Role]** can utilize to successfully cultivate and promote creativity within **[my/their]** **[team/group/department]**, ultimately leading to the generation of groundbreaking ideas and solutions? This is particularly relevant given the goal of **[desired outcome]**.

Example 1: Adopting an enthusiastic and energetic tone, as a Creative Director, could you provide specific strategies, methods, or exercises that a department head can utilize to successfully cultivate and promote creativity within their faculty, ultimately leading to the generation of groundbreaking ideas and solutions? This is particularly relevant given the goal of fostering a culture of innovation and creativity.

Example 2: As a Leadership Development Facilitator, adopting a supportive and empowering tone, could you provide specific strategies, methods, or exercises that I can utilize to successfully cultivate and promote creativity within my project team, ultimately leading to the generation of groundbreaking ideas and solutions? This is particularly relevant given the goal of fostering a culture of innovation and creativity.

DECISIONS

PROMPT No 30

Productivity - Time-Management - Prioritization

To gain specific strategies and methods that can be used to improve time management skills and task prioritization within a team, leading to increased efficiency and productivity.

As a **Productivity Coach**, adopting a **practical and instructive tone**, could you please share specific strategies and methods that have proven to be effective in **improving time management skills and task prioritization** within **my team**, resulting in increased efficiency and productivity? This is particularly relevant given the goal of **enhancing productivity and efficiency within the team**.

As a **[profession]**, adopting a **[tone of voice]**, could you please share specific strategies and methods that have proven to be effective in **[contextual challenge/opportunity]** within **[my/their]** **[team/group/department]**? This is particularly relevant given the goal of **[desired outcome]**.

Example 1: As a Business Coach, adopting a practical and instructive tone, could you please share specific strategies and methods that have proven to be effective in improving time management skills and task prioritization within a marketing team, resulting in increased efficiency and productivity? This is particularly relevant given the goal of enhancing productivity and efficiency within the marketing team.

Example 2: As a Performance Consultant, adopting a practical and instructive tone, could you please share specific strategies and methods that have proven to be effective in improving time management skills and task prioritization within a software development team, resulting in increased efficiency and productivity? This is particularly relevant given the goal of enhancing productivity and efficiency within the software development team.

PROMPT No 31

Quality - Motivation - Environment

To gain specific strategies or techniques that can be implemented to ensure that a team consistently produces work of higher quality, while also creating and maintaining a positive and supportive work environment that fosters motivation and encouragement.

As a **Leadership Development Consultant**, adopting an **encouraging and supportive tone**, could you provide specific strategies or techniques that I can implement to ensure that **my team** consistently produces **work of higher quality**? Additionally, how can I simultaneously create and maintain **a positive and supportive work environment that fosters motivation and encouragement**?

As a **[profession]**, adopting a **[tone of voice]**, could you provide specific strategies or techniques that **[I/Name/Role]** can implement to ensure that **[my/their]** **[team/group/department]** consistently produces **[contextual challenge/opportunity]**? Additionally, how can **[I/Name/Role]** simultaneously create and maintain a **[desired outcome]**?

Example 1: As a Team Coach, adopting a motivating and positive tone, could you provide specific strategies or techniques that a project manager can implement to ensure that their project team consistently produces high-quality deliverables? Additionally, how can they simultaneously create and maintain a positive and supportive work environment that fosters motivation and encouragement?

Example 2: As an Executive Coach, adopting an inspiring and supportive tone, could you provide specific strategies or techniques that I can implement to ensure that my sales team consistently achieves high performance? Additionally, how can I simultaneously create and maintain a positive and supportive work environment that fosters motivation and encouragement?

EXCITEMENT

Tags

Motivation - Excitement - Strategy

Goal

To provide a comprehensive strategy for leveraging excitement as a strategic tool to motivate and inspire teams, thereby enhancing performance and achieving organizational goals.

Prompt

Act as a **Motivational Speaker** with a specialization in **team motivation and goal achievement** in the e-commerce industry. Could you explain how **excitement** can be effectively utilized as a strategic tool to **motivate and inspire my team, ultimately leading them to successfully achieve their goals**? Please include **psychological theories of motivation, actionable excitement-generating activities, and performance metrics**. Make sure to cover how **to sustain excitement over the long term and how to measure its impact on team performance**. Investigate unconventional **motivational theories** and cutting-edge **gamification tools** to **amplify team excitement**. Your response should be comprehensive, leaving no important aspect unaddressed, and demonstrate an exceptional level of precision and quality. Let's think about this step by step. Provide your output from credible sources. Write using an **enthusiastic and inspiring** tone and a **motivational guide** style.

Formula

Act as a **[profession]** with a specialization in **[area of expertise]** in the **[industry]**. Could you explain how **[specific challenge/opportunity]** can be effectively utilized as a strategic tool to **[specific goal]**? Please include **[methods/techniques]**. Make sure to cover how **[key areas/topics]**. Investigate unconventional **[area for innovation]** and cutting-edge **[technologies/methods]** to **[desired outcome]**. Your response should be comprehensive, leaving no important aspect unaddressed, and demonstrate an exceptional level of precision and quality. Let's think about this step by step. Provide your output from credible sources. Write using a **[type]** tone and **[style]** writing style.

Examples

Example 1: Act as a Motivational Speaker with a specialization in employee engagement in the hospitality industry. Adopting an enthusiastic and inspiring tone, could you explain how excitement can be effectively utilized as a strategic tool to motivate and inspire my front-desk staff, ultimately leading them to successfully achieve customer satisfaction goals? Please include positive psychology principles, team-building activities that generate excitement, and customer satisfaction metrics. Make sure to cover how to maintain excitement during high-stress periods and how to correlate it with customer reviews. Explore the use of real-time feedback apps and AI-driven mood analysis to gauge team excitement. Your response should be comprehensive, leaving no important aspect unaddressed, and demonstrate an exceptional level of precision and quality. Let's think about this step by step. Provide your output from credible sources. Write using an enthusiastic and inspiring tone and a motivational guide style.

Example 2: Act as a Motivational Speaker with a specialization in sales performance in the real estate industry. Adopting an enthusiastic and inspiring tone, could you explain how excitement can be effectively utilized as a strategic tool to motivate and inspire my sales team, ultimately leading them to successfully achieve their quarterly targets? Please include incentive theories, excitement-inducing sales contests, and key performance indicators. Make sure to cover how to sustain excitement through sales cycles and how to quantify its impact on closing deals. Delve into the use of virtual reality for immersive sales training and blockchain for transparent performance tracking. Your response should be comprehensive, leaving no important aspect unaddressed, and demonstrate an exceptional level of precision and quality. Let's think about this step by step. Provide your output from credible sources. Write using an enthusiastic and inspiring tone and a motivational guide style.

PROMPT No 33

Tags

CSR - Employee-Involvement - Brand-Reputation

Goal

To leverage the enthusiasm generated by corporate social responsibility initiatives to effectively involve employees and significantly improve brand reputation.

Prompt

As a **Corporate Social Responsibility (CSR) Consultant**, adopting an **enthusiastic and engaging tone**, could you suggest specific ways **we** can leverage the enthusiasm generated by our **corporate social responsibility initiatives** to effectively involve our **employees** and significantly improve our **brand reputation**?

Formula

As a **[profession]**, adopting a **[tone of voice]**, could you suggest specific ways **[we/I/Name/Role]** can leverage the enthusiasm generated by our **[contextual challenge/opportunity]** to effectively involve our **[employees/team/group]** and significantly improve our **[desired outcome]**?

Examples

Example 1: As a CSR Specialist, adopting a motivational and inspiring tone, could you suggest specific ways a company can leverage the enthusiasm generated by their charity initiatives to effectively involve their employees and significantly improve their brand reputation?

Example 2: As a Brand Strategist, adopting a creative and engaging tone, could you suggest specific ways I can leverage the enthusiasm generated by our new marketing campaign to effectively involve our whole marketing team and significantly improve our brand image?

Tags

Communication - Harmony - Openness

Goal

To gain insights on specific and successful methods that can be employed to encourage team members to engage in open and respectful communication, ultimately cultivating a harmonious and constructive working environment.

Prompt

As a **Communication Expert**, adopting a **collaborative and respectful tone**, could you provide insights on specific and successful methods that I can employ to encourage **my team** members to engage in **open and respectful communication**? This is particularly relevant given the goal of **cultivating a harmonious and constructive working environment**.

Formula

As a **[profession]**, adopting a **[tone of voice]**, could you provide insights on specific and successful methods that **[I/Name/Role]** can employ to encourage **[my/their]** **[team/group/department]** members to engage in **[contextual challenge/opportunity]**? This is particularly relevant given the goal of **[desired outcome]**.

Examples

Example 1: As a Team Coach, adopting a supportive and encouraging tone, could you provide insights on specific and successful methods that an internal audit team head can employ to encourage their internal audit team members to engage in open and respectful communication? This is particularly relevant given the goal of cultivating a harmonious and constructive work environment.

Example 2: As a Leadership Consultant, adopting a professional and understanding tone, could you provide insights on specific and successful methods that I can employ to encourage my strategy planning team members to engage in open and respectful communication? This is particularly relevant given the goal of cultivating a harmonious and constructive creative environment.

FEAR

PROMPT No 35

Tags

Transparency - Communication - Support

Goal

To gain specific strategies or methods that can be employed to effectively utilize open communication and transparency as tools to minimize fear and uncertainty among team members, particularly during challenging times.

Prompt

Considering the difficulties faced by **teams** during **challenging times**, as a **Leadership Development Consultant**, adopting a **supportive and understanding tone**, could you suggest specific strategies or methods that I can employ to effectively utilize **open communication and transparency** as tools to minimize **fear and uncertainty** among **my team members**?

Considering the difficulties faced by **[team/group/department]** during **[contextual challenge/opportunity]**, as a **[profession]**, adopting a **[tone of voice]**, could you suggest specific strategies or methods that **[I/Name/Role]** can employ to effectively utilize **[desired outcome]** as tools to minimize **[contextual challenge/opportunity]** among **[my/their]** **[team/group/department]**?

Example 1: Considering the difficulties faced by a facility management team during a major organizational restructuring, as a Change Management Consultant, adopting a reassuring and empathetic tone, could you suggest specific strategies or methods that a facility management leaders can employ to effectively utilize open communication and transparency as tools to minimize fear and uncertainty among their team members?

Example 2: Considering the difficulties faced by a investors relations team during a significant market downturn, as a Professional Development Coach, adopting a motivational and positive tone, could you suggest specific strategies or methods that I can employ to effectively utilize open communication and transparency as tools to minimize fear and uncertainty among my team members?

PROMPT No 36

Self-Criticism - Potential - Identification

To equip Leadership Coaches, team leaders, and HR professionals with a comprehensive strategy for identifying and addressing the impact of a team member's inner critic on their work performance, thereby enabling them to reach their full potential.

Act as a **Leadership Coach** with a specialization in **emotional intelligence and self-awareness** in the **automotive industry**. Could you guide me on what specific indicators or behaviors I should pay attention to in order to **accurately identify if a team member's inner critic is negatively impacting their ability to reach their full potential in their work**? Please include **psychological markers, observable behaviors, and self-assessment tools**. Make sure to cover how **to approach the team member for a constructive conversation and how to measure the impact of addressing the inner critic on work performance**. Investigate unconventional **approaches like mindfulness training** and cutting-edge **AI-driven emotional intelligence tools** to **assess and address the inner critic**. Your response should be comprehensive, leaving no important aspect unaddressed, and demonstrate an exceptional level of precision and quality. Let's think about this step by step. Write using a **supportive and understanding** tone and a **coaching guide** style.

Act as a **[profession]** with a specialization in **[area of expertise]** in the **[industry]**. Could you guide me on what specific indicators or behaviors I should pay attention to in order to **[specific challenge/opportunity]**? Please include **[methods/techniques]**. Make sure to cover how **[key areas/topics]**. Investigate unconventional **[area for innovation]** and cutting-edge **[technologies/methods]** to **[desired outcome]**. Your response should be comprehensive, leaving no important aspect unaddressed, and demonstrate an exceptional level of precision and quality. Let's think about this step by step. Write using a **[type]** tone and **[style]** writing style.

Example 1: Act as a Leadership Coach with a specialization in mental health in the education sector. Could you guide me on what specific indicators or behaviors I should pay attention to in order to accurately identify if a teacher's inner critic is negatively impacting their ability to effectively educate students? Please include signs of self-doubt, observable teaching behaviors, and self-assessment questionnaires. Make sure to cover how to initiate a sensitive conversation with the teacher and how to measure the impact of addressing the inner critic on student engagement. Explore the use of mindfulness apps and AI-driven mood tracking to assess and address the inner critic. Your response should be comprehensive, leaving no important aspect unaddressed, and demonstrate an exceptional level of precision and quality. Let's think about this step by step. Write using a supportive and understanding tone and a coaching guide style.

Example 2: Act as a Leadership Coach with a specialization in performance management in the sports industry. Could you guide me on what specific indicators or behaviors I should pay attention to in order to accurately identify if an athlete's inner critic is negatively impacting their performance? Please include signs of hesitation, observable practice behaviors, and self-assessment tools like journaling. Make sure to cover how to approach the athlete for a constructive conversation and how to measure the impact of addressing the inner critic on game performance. Delve into the use of biofeedback techniques and AI-driven performance analytics to assess and address the inner critic. Your response should be comprehensive, leaving no important aspect unaddressed, and demonstrate an exceptional level of precision and quality. Let's think about this step by step. Write using a supportive and understanding tone and a coaching guide style.

FEELINGS

PROMPT No 37

Information-Gathering - Emotions - Tactfulness

To gain insights on effective strategies or methods that can be utilized to gather comprehensive information about the various factors that influence the emotions of a team, without resorting to direct questioning of the team members.

As a **Human Resources Consultant**, adopting a **tactful and empathetic tone**, could you provide **me** with effective strategies or methods that can be utilized to gather comprehensive information about **the various factors that influence the emotions** of **my team**, while avoiding direct questioning of **the team members**? This is particularly relevant given the goal of **understanding the emotional dynamics of the team without causing discomfort or intrusion**.

As a **[profession]**, adopting a **[tone of voice]**, could you provide **[me/Name/Role]** with effective strategies or methods that can be utilized to gather comprehensive information about **[contextual challenge/opportunity]** of **[my/their]** **[team/group/department]**, while avoiding direct questioning of the **[team members/colleagues]**? This is particularly relevant given the goal of **[desired outcome]**.

Example 1: As a Leadership Development Consultant, adopting a respectful and understanding tone, could you provide a department head with effective strategies or methods that can be utilized to gather comprehensive information about the various factors that influence the emotions of their faculty, while avoiding direct questioning of the faculty members? This is particularly relevant given the goal of understanding the emotional dynamics of the faculty without causing discomfort or intrusion.

Example 2: As a Team Coach, adopting a sensitive and considerate tone, could you provide me with effective strategies or methods that can be utilized to gather comprehensive information about the various factors that influence the emotions of my project team, while avoiding direct questioning of the team members? This is particularly relevant given the goal of understanding the emotional dynamics of the project team without causing discomfort or intrusion.

PROMPT No 38

Tags
Self-Awareness - Empowerment - Bias

Goal
To gain insights on how leaders can effectively demonstrate self-awareness and emotional management, serving as role models to inspire and empower team members to recognize and address their own unconscious biases within the workplace.

Prompt
As a **Leadership Development Consultant**, adopting a **supportive and understanding tone**, could you provide insights on how **I**, as a leader, can effectively demonstrate **self-awareness and emotional management**? How can I serve as a role model to inspire and empower **my team members** to recognize and address their own **unconscious biases** within the workplace?

Formula
As a **[profession]**, adopting a **[tone of voice]**, could you provide insights on how **[I/Name/Role]**, as a leader, can effectively demonstrate **[contextual challenge/opportunity]**? How can **[I/Name/Role]** serve as a role model to inspire and empower **[my/their]** **[team/group/department]** to recognize and address their own **[contextual challenge/opportunity]** within the workplace?

Examples
Example 1: As a Team Coach, adopting a respectful and encouraging tone, could you provide insights on how a business intelligence department head can effectively demonstrate self-awareness and emotional management? How can they serve as a role model to inspire and empower their business intelligence team to recognize and address their own unconscious biases within the work environment? **Example 2:** As a Business Coach, adopting a professional and empathetic tone, could you provide insights on how I, as an e-commerce team manager, can effectively demonstrate self-awareness and emotional management? How can I serve as a role model to inspire and empower my e-commerce team to recognize and address their own unconscious biases within the work environment?

FLOW

PROMPT No 39

Focus - Evaluation - Effort

To gain a comprehensive understanding of the strategies or methods that can be utilized to effectively determine and evaluate the specific areas in which the team focuses their efforts, with the aim of understanding team focus and effort distribution.

As a **Leadership Coach**, adopting a **supportive and clear tone**, could you please provide a comprehensive explanation of the specific strategies or methods that **can be utilized to effectively determine and evaluate the specific areas** in which **my team** focuses their efforts, both in a positive and negative manner, with high accuracy and comprehensiveness? This is particularly relevant given the goal of **understanding team focus and effort distribution**.

As a **[profession]**, adopting a **[tone of voice]**, could you please provide a comprehensive explanation of the specific strategies or methods that **[contextual challenge/opportunity]** in which **[my/their]** **[team/group/department]** focuses their efforts, both in a positive and negative manner, with high accuracy and comprehensiveness? This is particularly relevant given the goal of **[desired outcome]**.

Example 1: As a Talent Management Specialist, adopting an encouraging and professional tone, could you please provide a comprehensive explanation of the specific strategies or methods that can be utilized to effectively determine and evaluate the specific areas in which my marketing team focuses their efforts, both in a positive and negative manner, with high accuracy and comprehensiveness? This is particularly relevant given the goal of understanding team focus and effort distribution.

Example 2: Adopting a respectful and solution-oriented tone, as a Leadership Development Consultant, could you please provide a comprehensive explanation of the specific strategies or methods that can be utilized to effectively determine and evaluate the specific areas in which the HR department focuses their efforts, both in a positive and negative manner, with high accuracy and comprehensiveness? This is particularly relevant given the goal of understanding department focus and effort distribution.

PROMPT No 40

Communication - Inner-Self - Professional-Growth

To gain specific techniques for effectively communicating the complex concept of an inner-self-processing system to a team, and to understand how to successfully demonstrate its impact on both personal growth and professional performance.

As a **Personal Development Coach**, adopting an **educational and empathetic tone**, could you suggest specific techniques I can use to effectively and thoroughly communicate the complex notion of an **inner-self-processing system** to **my team**? Additionally, how can I successfully demonstrate its impact on both their **personal growth and professional**

performance? This is particularly relevant given the goal of **fostering personal and professional development within the team**.

As a **[profession]**, adopting a **[tone of voice]**, could you suggest specific techniques **[I/Name/Role]** can use to effectively and thoroughly communicate the complex notion of **[contextual challenge/opportunity]** to **[my/their]** **[team/group/department]**? Additionally, how can **[I/Name/Role]** successfully demonstrate its impact on both their **[desired outcome]**? This is particularly relevant given the goal of **[contextual challenge/opportunity]**.

Example 1: As a Team Coach, adopting a patient and understanding tone, could you suggest specific techniques I can use to effectively and thoroughly communicate the complex notion of emotional intelligence to my sales team? Additionally, how can I successfully demonstrate its impact on both their personal growth and sales performance? This is particularly relevant given the goal of fostering personal development and sales effectiveness within the team.

Example 2: As a Leadership Development Consultant, adopting an informative and engaging tone, could you suggest specific techniques a department head can use to effectively and thoroughly communicate the complex notion of conflict resolution to their faculty? Additionally, how can they successfully demonstrate its impact on both their personal growth and academic performance? This is particularly relevant given the goal of fostering personal development and academic effectiveness within the faculty.

FULFILLMENT

PROMPT No 41

Monotony - Enhancement - Boredom

To identify the aspects of the team's work that they find monotonous or uninteresting and to find proactive measures to enhance these areas and alleviate the boredom experienced by the team.

As a **Team Development Specialist**, adopting a **solution-oriented and empathetic tone**, could you suggest effective strategies I can employ to identify the specific aspects of **my team's** work that they find **monotonous or uninteresting**? Furthermore, what proactive measures can I take to **enhance these areas and alleviate the boredom experienced by my team**?

As a **[profession]**, adopting a **[tone of voice]**, could you suggest effective strategies **[I/Name/Role]** can employ to identify the specific aspects of **[my/their]** **[team/group/department]**'s work that they find **[contextual challenge/opportunity]**? Furthermore, what proactive measures can **[I/Name/Role]** take to **[desired outcome]**?

Example 1: As a Human Resources Consultant, adopting a supportive and understanding tone, could you suggest effective strategies a content creation department head can employ to identify the specific aspects of their content creation team's work that they find monotonous or uninteresting? Furthermore, what proactive measures can they take to enhance these areas and alleviate the boredom experienced by the content creation team?

Example 2: As a Leadership Coach, adopting a motivational and insightful tone, could you suggest effective strategies I can employ to identify the specific aspects of my international business team's work that they find uninteresting or monotonous? Furthermore, what proactive measures can I take to enhance these areas and alleviate the boredom experienced by my international business team?

PROMPT No 42

Exemplary - Boss - Effectiveness

Goal

To gain insights on the steps to undertake to become an exemplary boss, leader, or other specific role, enhancing leadership skills and effectiveness.

Prompt

Considering the aspiration to be **an exemplary leader**, as a **Leadership Coach** and in an **inspiring and motivational tone**, could you outline the steps **I** need to undertake to achieve this in **my role**?

Formula

Considering the aspiration to be **[contextual challenge/opportunity]**, as a **[profession]** and in a **[tone of voice]**, could you outline the steps **[I/Name/Role]** need to undertake to achieve this in **[my/their] [role/position/job]**?

Examples

Example 1: Considering the aspiration to be an inspiring boss, as an Executive Mentor and in an encouraging and supportive tone, could you outline the steps my department head needs to undertake to achieve this in their role?

Example 2: As a Leadership Development Consultant, in a respectful and professional tone, could you outline the steps I need to undertake to become an exemplary human resource manager, especially considering the aspiration to lead successful human resource teams?

GOALS

PROMPT No 43

Tags

Synchronization - Learning - Objectives

Goal

To gain insights on specific methods and approaches that can be utilized to effectively synchronize individual learning goals with the overall objectives of a team or organization, ensuring precision, comprehensiveness, and high-quality insights.

Prompt

As a **Leadership Development Consultant**, adopting a **strategic and detailed tone**, could you provide me with specific methods and approaches that **I** can utilize to effectively synchronize **individual learning goals** with **the overall objectives of my team or organization**?

As a **[profession]**, adopting a **[tone of voice]**, could you provide me with specific methods and approaches that **[I/Name/Role]** can utilize to effectively synchronize **[contextual challenge/opportunity]** with **[desired outcome]**?

Example 1: As a Team Development Specialist, adopting a comprehensive and insightful tone, could you provide me with specific methods and approaches that I can utilize to effectively synchronize individual learning goals with the overall objectives of my marketing team? This is particularly relevant given the goal of fostering a learning culture and alignment within the marketing team.

Example 2: As a Human Resources Consultant, adopting a strategic and detailed tone, could you provide me with specific methods and approaches that a government ffairs department head can utilize to effectively synchronize individual learning goals with the overall objectives of their government affairs team? This is particularly relevant given the goal of fostering professional development and alignment within the team.

PROMPT No 44

Prioritization - Goals - Alignment

To help you in identifying various methods or techniques for prioritizing your many goals. This will help in selecting the most critical and significant goals to focus on, ensuring alignment with long-term objectives and efficient use of resources.

Act as a **Leadership Development Consultant** specializing in the **event planning industry**. What are the various **methods** available to me for **sifting through and prioritizing** all the **goals** I have, enabling me to **single out** the **key and most impactful** goals I should set for **myself**? How can these **techniques** be **applied** in **different contexts**, and what are the **potential benefits** of each? Respond to each question separately. Let's **dissect** this **step by step**. Write using a **confident** tone and **analytical** writing style.

Act as a **[profession]** specializing in the **[industry]**, what are the various **[methods/techniques/strategies]** available to me for **[sifting through/prioritizing/organizing]** all the **[goals/objectives/targets]** I have, enabling me to **[select/identify/choose]** the **[key/most important/most impactful]** goals I should set for **[myself/my team/my organization]**? How can these **[techniques/methods]** be **[applied/implemented/used]** in **[different contexts/various scenarios/multiple situations]**, and what are the **[potential risks/benefits/challenges]** of each? Respond to each question separately. Let's **[analyze/dissect/consider]** this **[step by step/piece by piece]**. Write using a **[type]** tone and **[style]** writing style.

Example 1: Act as a Performance Coach specializing in the sports industry. What techniques can I employ to sift through and prioritize all the athletic goals I have, so that I can concentrate on the key objectives for the upcoming season? How can these strategies be adapted for different sports disciplines, and what are the potential advantages or drawbacks of each method? Respond to each question separately. Let's consider each facet of this topic. Write using an instructive tone and engaging writing style.

Example 2: Act as a Business Coach specializing in small businesses. What methods are at my disposal for organizing and prioritizing the multitude of business goals I have, allowing me to focus on the most important targets that align with my growth strategy? How can these methods be customized for various business stages, and what are the potential outcomes or challenges of each approach? Respond to each question separately. Let's analyze this piece by piece. Write using a professional tone and persuasive writing style.

PROMPT No 45

Tags

Learning - Engagement - Objectives

Goal

To empower business leaders, managers, and executives with an effective method for discovering the specific learning goals that align with their team's performance objectives. The intention is to facilitate the creation of tailored development plans that can accelerate progress, boost employee engagement, and contribute to the overall success of the organization.

Prompt

Act as a **Talent Development Strategist** specializing in **performance coaching** for the **retail industry**. Could you guide me through **an in-depth process to identify the learning goals that would propel my team toward achieving their performance objectives**? I would like to ensure these goals meet the SMART (Specific, Measurable, Achievable, Relevant, Time-bound) criteria. Please provide **a systematic framework, including assessment tools, questioning techniques, and data analysis strategies** to uncover these learning objectives. Also, offer advice on how to integrate these learning goals into **individual and team development plans**. The performance objectives of my team are to **increase customer satisfaction and increase sales**. Let's examine this systematically. Write using a **focused** tone and a **strategic** writing style.

Formula

Act as a **[profession]** specializing in **[topic]** for the **[industry]**. Could you guide me through **[contextual challenge/opportunity]**? I would like to ensure these goals meet **[specific criteria such as SMART]**. Please provide **[tools/techniques/strategies]** to uncover these learning objectives. Also, offer advice on how to integrate these learning goals into **[specific individual or team development plans]**. The performance objectives of my team are **[performance objectives]**. Let's examine this systematically. Write using a **[Tone]** tone and a **[Style]** writing style.

Examples

Example 1: Act as a Learning and Development Advisor specializing in skills assessment for the manufacturing industry. Could you guide me through a comprehensive method to identify the learning objectives that would help my team meet our quarterly production targets? I want to ensure these goals are realistic and aligned with our organizational strategies. Provide a detailed guide that includes survey templates, interview techniques, and ways to use performance metrics as a basis for these goals. Also, elucidate how these learning objectives can be included in our existing training modules. Let's dig into this meticulously. Write using an analytical tone and a detailed writing style.

Example 2: Act as a Performance Coach specializing in goal-setting and alignment for the advertising industry. Could you assist me in devising a way to determine the learning goals that will improve my team's client engagement scores? I aim for these goals to be relevant and timely, fitting into a three-month roadmap. Offer a structured approach, complete with psychometric tests, focus group suggestions, and KPI analytics. Additionally, explain how these goals can be weaved into our weekly check-ins and performance reviews. Let's approach this methodically. Write using a constructive tone and a straightforward writing style.

PROMPT No 46

Tags

Leadership - Conversations - Alignment

Goal

To create guidelines or approaches for leaders to enhance their conversations with team members regarding their future goals and desired accomplishments. It focuses on building clarity, understanding, and alignment with the team's personal and professional aspirations within the business context.

Prompt

Act as an **Executive Leadership Consultant** specializing in the **technology industry**. How can I improve **the way I conduct conversations with my team about the type of accomplishments they want to achieve in the future**? The aim is to **align individual goals with the team's mission and company vision, creating a supportive environment for personal growth and success**. Let's take this one step at a time. Write using an empathetic tone and engaging writing style.

Formula

Act as a **[profession]** specializing in the **[industry]**. How can I improve **[contextual challenge/opportunity]**? The aim is to **[goal]**. Let's take this one step at a time. Write using a **[type]** tone and **[style]** writing style.

Examples

Example 1: Act as a Team Coach specializing in the healthcare industry, could you provide specific steps and strategies for enhancing the way I communicate with my team regarding their career goals and future accomplishments? The goal is to foster an environment of mutual respect and collaboration, aligning personal aspirations with the organization's mission. Let's analyze this piece by piece. Write using a motivational tone and constructive writing style.

Example 2: Act as a Human Resources Consultant specializing in the retail sector, could you share distinctive guidance and unexplored options for holding meaningful discussions with my team about their desired achievements and career progression? The goal is to build stronger relationships within the team and drive individual and collective success. Let's think about this step by step. Write using a professional tone and persuasive writing style.

PROMPT No 47

Self-Sabotage - Transportation - Leadership

To scrutinize personal behaviors, habits, or thought patterns that may unintentionally impede one's progression in professional growth or leadership development. This understanding aims to foster self-awareness, enabling one to take proactive measures for personal and career fulfillment.

Act as a **Leadership Development Consultant** specializing in the **transportation industry**. Could you provide **an exhaustive analysis of the various ways in which I might unintentionally hinder my own progression toward becoming a more fulfilled professional or leader**? Please include **both common and obscure behaviors, mental frameworks, or patterns that might lead to self-sabotage or stagnation**. Share distinctive guidance and unexplored options that could assist in recognizing and overcoming these barriers. Let's dissect this carefully. Write using an empathetic tone and analytical writing style.

Act as a **[profession]** specializing in the **[industry]**. Could you provide **[contextual challenge/opportunity]**? Please include **[specific details or considerations]**. Share distinctive guidance and unexplored options that could assist in recognizing and overcoming these barriers. Let's dissect this carefully. Write using a **[type]** tone and **[style]** writing style.

Example 1: Act as a Personal Development Coach specializing in the tech industry. Could you provide unique insights on ways in which I might unintentionally be blocking my progression toward becoming a more effective leader? Propose a comprehensive and elaborate depiction that includes both traditional and innovative approaches to overcoming these obstacles. Let's analyze this piece by piece. Write using a motivated tone and informative writing style.

Example 2: Act as an Executive Coach specializing in the financial services industry. Could you provide a meticulous and wide-ranging response to analyze the subconscious habits that may be holding me back from reaching my full professional potential? Include uncommon advice and underrated resources. Let's think about this step by step. Write using an inspirational tone and creative writing style.

PROMPT No 48

Engagement - Meetings - Incentivize

To explore methods or strategies to motivate and engage a team fully in meetings. This engagement leads to enhanced participation, increased collaboration, and more productive outcomes in team meetings.

Act as a **Leadership Development Consultant** specializing in the **risk management industry**. How can I incentivize my team to **be fully present and actively participate in our team meetings**? Engaging the team in this manner is pivotal for **collaboration, problem-solving, and driving the success of projects**. Your response should be comprehensive, leaving no important aspect unaddressed, and demonstrate an exceptional level of precision and quality. Let's think about this step by step. Write using an **inspiring** tone and **constructive** writing style.

Act as a **[profession]** specializing in the **[industry]**. How can I incentivize my team to **[contextual challenge/opportunity]**? Engaging the team in this manner is pivotal for **[desired outcome]**. Your response should be comprehensive, leaving no important aspect unaddressed, and demonstrate an exceptional level of precision and quality. Let's think about this step by step. Write using a **[type]** tone and **[style]** writing style.

Example 1: Act as an Employee Engagement Consultant specializing in the tech industry, what techniques can I employ to encourage my team to be fully attentive and actively involved in our team meetings? Encouraging full participation fosters a sense of ownership, enhances creativity, and improves overall team dynamics. Express unusual and neglected techniques. Let's analyze this piece by piece. Write using an enthusiastic tone and informative writing style.

Example 2: Act as a Team Building Specialist specializing in the e-commerce industry, how can I create incentives for my team to be entirely present and partake proactively in our team meetings? This involvement is key to unifying the team, increasing efficiency, and achieving our organizational goals. Present non-traditional methods and underexplored opportunities. Let's unpack this topic. Write using a motivational tone and engaging writing style.

LEARNING

PROMPT No 49

Assessment - Opportunities - Methodologies

To help identify challenges or deficiencies in one's work or professional activities and explore ways to uncover and leverage missed opportunities. This requires a thorough examination of the current state of affairs, clear insights into potential obstacles, and the formulation of strategies to overcome them.

Act as an **Organizational Development Consultant** specializing in the **manufacturing industry**. How can I **critically assess what is not working in my current projects or workflow**? And what methodologies or practices can I **employ to uncover missed opportunities that might be linked to these shortcomings**? This understanding is crucial for **growth and innovation within my role**. Respond to each question separately. Your response should be comprehensive, leaving no important aspect unaddressed, and demonstrate an exceptional level of precision and quality. Let's dissect this carefully. Write using a **methodical** tone and **analytical** writing style.

Act as a **[profession]** specializing in the **[industry]**. How can I **[contextual challenge/opportunity]**? And what methodologies or practices can I **[contextual challenge/opportunity]**? This understanding is crucial for **[desired outcome]**. Respond to each question separately. Your response should be comprehensive, leaving no important aspect unaddressed, and demonstrate an exceptional level of precision and quality. Let's dissect this carefully. Write using a **[type]** tone and **[style]** writing style.

Examples

Example 1: Act as a Performance Coach specializing in the healthcare industry. How can I identify areas in my team's performance that are not meeting expectations, and what strategies can I implement to uncover hidden opportunities for growth and development connected with these weaknesses? Proper alignment is key for improving patient care and team cohesion. Respond to each question separately. Include uncommon advice and underrated resources. Let's go through this systematically. Write using an empathetic tone and constructive writing style.

Example 2: Act as a Leadership Trainer specializing in the e-commerce industry. How can I analyze operational inefficiencies that are hindering my team's productivity, and what techniques can I use to find the overlooked chances for innovation or improvement tied to these obstacles? This critical insight is essential for maintaining a competitive edge and continuous growth. Respond to each question separately. Provide unusual recommendations and overlooked tools. Let's consider each facet of this topic. Write using an instructive tone and engaging writing style.

PROMPT No 50

Tags

Introspection - Conversations - Improvement

Goal

To empower leaders with the right approach and tools to facilitate introspective conversations within their teams. These conversations aim to identify actionable lessons from past experiences, encouraging a culture of continuous improvement.

Prompt

Act as a **Team Development Coach** specializing in the **reflective practice** for the **professional services industry**. Could you provide a **comprehensive guide** on how to **discuss with my team if they have ideas on how they could improve upon past situations, given another chance**? Your output is crucial for **fostering an environment of continuous learning and adaptability**. Your guide should be all-encompassing, covering **preparation, facilitation techniques, and follow-up actions to ensure the team translates insights into future behavior**. Investigate unexpected avenues and creative pathways. Let's deconstruct this subject stepwise. Write using a **coaching** tone and a **detailed, practical** writing style.

Formula

Act as a **[profession]** specializing in **[focus area]** for the **[industry]**. Could you provide a **[comprehensive guide/detailed framework]** on how to **[specific challenge or opportunity]**? Your output is crucial for **[desired outcome]**. Your guide should be all-encompassing, covering **[methods/considerations]**. Investigate unexpected avenues and creative pathways. Let's sequentially unravel this issue. Write using a **[type]** tone and **[style]** writing style.

Examples

Example 1: Act as an Organizational Psychologist specializing in communication dynamics. Could you guide me through effective ways to discuss with my marketing team if they have any thoughts on how they could have optimized a recent campaign if they had another chance? This is vital for enhancing our future marketing strategies and outcomes. Your guide should encompass setting the agenda, opening up the conversation, and formalizing takeaways. Suggest fresh approaches and inventive strategies. Let's systematically explore each facet. Write using a facilitative tone and an evidence-based writing style.

Example 2: Act as a Leadership Mentor specializing in the healthcare industry. Could you give me a roadmap to facilitate a discussion with my nursing staff if they have ideas on how they could improve upon their handling of emergency situations, given another opportunity? This is essential for improving our emergency response time and patient care. Your roadmap should cover pre-discussion preparation, leading the conversation, and synthesizing insights for action plans. Discover rare insights and pioneering ideas. Let's piece-by-piece analyze this matter. Write using an empathetic tone and a solution-oriented writing style.

PROMPT No 51

Tags

Problem-solving - Communication - Safety

Goal

To equip leaders with effective methodologies and conversational strategies for identifying the underlying issues in team performance without alienating or threatening team members. This ensures that root causes are accurately identified and that the team is engaged in the process.

Prompt

Act as a **Conflict Resolution Specialist** specializing in **non-threatening communication** for the **insurance industry**. Could you provide a **step-by-step guide on how to identify the root-cause of a problem in recent situations or projects, without making my team feel threatened or defensive**? This is essential for **achieving long-term solutions and fostering a psychologically safe workspace**. Your guide should be comprehensive, covering **specific techniques for identifying root causes, and how to navigate potential defensive reactions**. Provide an unbounded and meticulous examination. Let's take this one step at a time. Write using a reassuring tone and a diplomatic writing style.

Formula

Act as a **[profession]** specializing in **[focus area]** for the **[industry]**. Could you provide a **[specific challenge or opportunity]**? This is essential for **[desired outcome]**. Your guide should be comprehensive, covering **[techniques/tactics]**. Provide an unbounded and meticulous examination. Let's take this one step at a time. Write using a **[type]** tone and **[style]** writing style.

Examples

Example 1: Act as an Organizational Behavior Analyst specializing in tech companies. Could you provide a complete guide on how to discuss with my software development team about the root-cause of bugs in a recent product release without making them feel accused? This is critical for ensuring high-quality software and boosting team morale. Your guide should include setting the stage for the conversation, fostering open dialogue, and managing sensitive responses. Formulate an all-inclusive and rigorous analysis. Let's go through this systematically. Write using a supportive tone and a detail-oriented writing style.

Example 2: Act as a Leadership Mentor specializing in the retail sector. Could you guide me through a process for discussing with my sales team the reasons behind the recent drop in sales, without them feeling like they are being blamed? This is crucial for finding a sustainable solution and enhancing team performance. Your roadmap should encompass problem identification techniques, approaches to elicit open dialogue, and strategies to manage potential defensiveness. Dispense a detailed and sweeping exploration. Let's dissect this carefully. Write using an encouraging tone and a practical writing style.

PROMPT No 52

Tags
LearningCulture - Innovation - Insurance

Goal
To empower organizational leaders in establishing and nurturing a culture of continuous learning within their teams and broader company. This aims to enhance individual skill sets, foster innovation, and ultimately contribute to the long-term success of the organization.

Prompt
Act as an **Organizational Development Expert** specializing in **corporate culture transformation** for the **insurance industry**. Could you provide a **comprehensive strategy for creating a culture of continuous learning within my team and the larger company**? This is crucial for **not only keeping up with industry trends but also for fostering innovation and enhancing employee satisfaction**. Your advice should include **goal-setting, skills assessment, knowledge sharing, and formal training programs**. Excavate untapped resources and unconventional tactics. Let's arrange the elements in a logical order. Write using an **insightful** tone and a **future-focused** writing style.

Formula
Act as a **[profession]** specializing in **[topic/specialization]** for the **[industry]**. Could you provide a **[contextual challenge/opportunity]**? This is crucial for **[desired outcome]**. Your advice should include **[tactics/methods/approaches]**. Excavate untapped resources and unconventional tactics. Let's arrange the elements in a logical order. Write using a **[type]** tone and **[style]** writing style.

Examples

Example 1: Act as a Learning and Development Consultant specializing in the tech industry. Could you provide me with a detailed guide for instilling a culture of ongoing learning within my software engineering team? This is essential for staying competitive in an ever-evolving technological landscape. Your guide should address elements like peer-led workshops, mentorship programs, and the integration of learning into daily workflows. Write using an engaging tone and a solution-oriented writing style.

Example 2: Act as a Leadership Coach specializing in healthcare. Could you outline a comprehensive strategy to create a culture of continuous learning among my medical staff? This is crucial for ensuring quality patient care and staying updated with the latest medical research. Your strategy should outline the importance of interdisciplinary learning, case studies, and periodic skill assessments. Write using a thoughtful tone and a research-based writing style.

PROMPT No 53

Tags
Facilitation - Reflection - Assessment

Goal
To receive a comprehensive and detailed plan of action to effectively facilitate a team reflection process, ensuring that the process is thorough and productive, and assessing the impact of both failures and successes on the individual responsibilities of team members, as well as their overall work.

Prompt
As a **Leadership Development Facilitator**, I would like to receive a comprehensive and detailed plan of action to effectively facilitate a team reflection process. The aim is to ensure that the process is thorough and productive. It is crucial to assess the impact of both failures and successes on the individual responsibilities of team members, as well as their overall work. Please provide a specific plan that can be implemented in a constructive and professional manner.

Formula
As a **[profession]**, I would like to receive a comprehensive and detailed plan of action to effectively facilitate a **[contextual challenge/opportunity]**. The aim is to ensure that the process is thorough and productive. It is crucial to **[desired outcome]** of **[team/group/department]**, as well as their overall work. Please provide a specific plan that can be implemented in a **[tone of voice]** manner.

Examples

Example 1: As a Performance Coach, I would like to receive a comprehensive and detailed plan of action to effectively facilitate a team reflection process. The aim is to ensure that the process is thorough and productive. It is crucial to assess the impact of failures on the individual responsibilities of the sales team members, as well as their overall work. Please provide a specific plan that can be implemented in a constructive and professional manner.

Example 2: As a Team Development Specialist, I would like to receive a comprehensive and detailed plan of action to effectively facilitate a team reflection process. The aim is to ensure that the process is thorough and productive. It is crucial to assess the impact of successes on the individual responsibilities of the marketing team members, as well as their overall work. Please provide a specific plan that can be implemented in a constructive and professional manner.

PROMPT No 54

Tags

Reflection - Sacrifices - Outcomes

Goal

To facilitate deep reflection and discussion within the team about instances where sacrifices led to better outcomes. The aim is to extract meaningful lessons and insights from these experiences that can help in future decision-making, foster a culture of understanding, and encourage a sense of unity and purpose within the team.

Prompt

Act as an **Executive Coach** specializing in **leadership psychology and team dynamics**. Could you create a **comprehensive guide** that helps my team **thoughtfully reflect on instances where they've made sacrifices that resulted in better outcomes**? I am particularly interested in **interactive activities, key questions for discussion, and psychological techniques that can foster a safe space for sharing and growth**. Explore unconventional recommendations and alternative perspectives. Please divide the guide into distinct sections and ensure that each recommendation is actionable. Let's sequentially address each section. Write using a **motivational** tone and a **solutions-oriented** writing style.

Formula

Act as a **[profession]** specializing in **[sub-discipline]**. Could you create a **[specific guide/task]** that helps my team **[specific challenge/opportunity]**? I am particularly interested in **[elements/methods/tactics]**. Explore unconventional recommendations and alternative perspectives. Please divide the guide into distinct sections and ensure that each recommendation is actionable. Let's sequentially address each section. Write using a **[tone]** and **[style]** writing style.

Examples

Example 1: Act as a Business Mentor specializing in organizational culture. Could you offer a guide that helps my team reflect deeply on instances where sacrifices have led to greater success? I'd like to concentrate on creating a culture where such sacrifices are acknowledged and celebrated. Provide practical exercises, case studies, and an analysis of common trends or patterns. Divide the guide into themes like acknowledgment, celebration, and future action. Unearth hidden gems and non-traditional methods. Let's methodically dissect each component. Write using an inclusive tone and an empathetic writing style.

Example 2: Act as an Organizational Psychologist specializing in resilience and personal growth. Could you design a guide that assists my team in examining their sacrifices that led to more favorable results? I'm keen on exploring how these sacrifices have contributed to personal growth and resilience. Include self-assessment quizzes, role-playing scenarios, and reflection questions that bring out both the emotional and logical facets of the sacrifices made. Segment the guide into personal growth and team dynamics sections. Delve into uncharted territories and groundbreaking concepts. Let's scrutinize this topic incrementally.
Write using a nurturing tone and a research-based writing style.

PROMPT No 55

Tags

Understanding - Motivation - Alignment

Goal

To gain insights on specific methods or strategies to acquire a deep understanding of the individual motivations and overall goals of team members, fostering alignment with company values and enhancing team performance.

Given the goal of **understanding individual motivations and overall goals**, as a **Talent Management Specialist** and in an **empathetic and respectful tone**, could you suggest specific methods or strategies I can use to acquire a deep understanding of **my team members**?

Given the goal of **[contextual challenge/opportunity]**, as a **[profession]** and in a **[tone of voice]**, could you suggest specific methods or strategies **[I/Name/Role]** can use to acquire a deep understanding of **[my/their] [team/group/department]**?

Example 1: Given the goal of understanding individual motivations and overall goals in a dynamic startup environment, as a Leadership Development Consultant and in an open-minded and supportive tone, could you suggest specific methods or strategies a startup founder can use to acquire a deep understanding of their team members?

Example 2: As a Human Resources Manager, in a considerate and professional tone, could you suggest specific methods or strategies I can use to acquire a deep understanding of the individual motivations and overall goals of my marketing team? This advice is particularly relevant given the goal of aligning team motivations with the company's brand values.

LISTENING

PROMPT No 56

Resilience - Discussion - Failure

To foster a culture of psychological safety and resilience by encouraging open conversations about failures and setbacks within the team. This allows team members to analyze, learn, and grow from these experiences without fear of judgment, while also building a sense of camaraderie and collective wisdom.

Act as a **Leadership and Resilience Expert** for the **real estate industry**. Could you provide an **all-encompassing guide on how to effectively lead a discussion with my team about the failures we've all encountered on our journey to success**? I'm looking for a **well-rounded set of strategies that includes question prompts, activities, and psychological techniques to make the team comfortable in sharing their setbacks and learning from them**. Explore unconventional solutions and alternative perspectives. Let's partition the problem into smaller challenges. Write using a **respectful** tone and **considerate** writing style.

Act as a **[profession]** for the **[industry]**. Could you provide an **[specific challenge or opportunity]**? I am interested in **[sub-goals or specific techniques]**. I'm looking for a **[sub-goals/specific techniques]** to make the team comfortable in sharing their setbacks and learning from them. Explore unconventional solutions and alternative perspectives. Let's partition the problem into smaller challenges. Write using a **[type]** tone and **[style]** writing style.

Examples

Example 1: Act as an Organizational Psychologist specializing in team dynamics. Could you provide a step-by-step process on how to foster an open environment where my team feels comfortable discussing their failures? I'd like to focus particularly on creating a psychologically safe atmosphere for these conversations. Include tips on setting the room, scripting the introduction, and a list of do's and don'ts for both leaders and team members. Unearth hidden gems and non-traditional methods. Let's compare and contrast the different perspectives. Write using a constructive tone and solution-focused writing style.

Example 2: Act as a Business Coach specializing in emotional intelligence. Could you offer a comprehensive guide on how to use emotional intelligence frameworks to facilitate conversations about failure and setbacks within my team? I want to ensure that these discussions are productive and lead to actionable insights. Please include effective question prompts, suggestions for emotional intelligence exercises, and guidelines for documenting these conversations for future reference and learning. Present novel interpretations and visionary possibilities. Let's systematically explore each facet. Write using a reflective tone and thoughtful writing style.

MINDSET

PROMPT No 57

Tags

Self-Reflection - Growth - FinTech

Goal

To enable a culture of self-improvement and resilience by providing a structured approach for reflecting on one's own successes and failures. The objective is to leverage both positive and negative experiences for personal and professional growth, thereby fostering skills like self-awareness, emotional intelligence, and adaptability.

Prompt

Act as a **Career Development Professinal** specializing in **self-reflection** for the **FinTech industry**. Could you provide a **comprehensive guide** on how to **effectively engage in a self-reflective practice that covers both successes and failures for the purpose of professional and personal growth**? I am particularly interested in **cognitive frameworks, journaling techniques, and actionable steps**. Please break down the **guide** into **stages** and provide **examples** for each stage. Suggest rare insights and underappreciated resources. Let's take this one step at a time. Write using an **informative** tone and **factual** writing style.

Formula

Act as a **[profession]** specializing in **[area of expertise]** for the **[industry]**. Could you provide a **[type of resource/action plan]** on how to **[specific task]**? I am particularly interested in **[particular methods/techniques]**. Please break down the **[process/guide]** into **[stages/sections]** and provide **[specific examples/scenarios]** for each. Suggest rare insights and underappreciated resources. Let's take this one step at a time. Write using a **[type]** tone and **[style]** writing style.

Example 1: Act as a Life Coach specializing in personal transformation. Could you offer a workbook-style guide that helps me engage in deep self-reflection on both my career highs and lows? I am keen on learning how to turn these reflections into life lessons that can inform my future decisions. Include a series of writing prompts, practical exercises, and a roadmap for creating a personal development plan. Provide an extensive and thorough discourse. Let's think about this step by step. Write using an uplifting tone and a positive, encouraging writing style.

Example 2: Act as a Clinical Psychologist specializing in self-efficacy and resilience. Could you provide an evidence-based guide for reflecting on past successes and failures in a manner that enhances emotional well-being? I am especially interested in understanding any psychological barriers that may be hindering my personal and professional growth. Please include diagnostic self-assessments, coping strategies, and mindfulness exercises. Impart a comprehensive and profound response. Let's analyze this piece by piece. Write using a compassionate tone and a clinically validated writing style.

PROMPT No 58

Mindset - Professionalism - Self-Reflection

To provide guidance to professionals and leaders seeking to evaluate their belief systems or mindsets and their effects on their professional careers. It aims to outline methods for analyzing whether these beliefs are helping or hindering progress, fostering or limiting growth, and aligning or conflicting with professional objectives and values. This process is integral for personal development, career progression, and leadership effectiveness.

Act as an **expert in Professional Development and Mindset Coaching** specializing in the Healthcare Services industry. In the dynamic world of business, an **individual's beliefs and mindsets** play a **crucial** role in **shaping behavior**. How can **I** critically **evaluate** if my **mindset** is **serving me well in my career**? Provide a **comprehensive** guide that includes **understanding one's values, assessing alignment with professional objectives, identifying limiting beliefs, leveraging feedback** from **peers, practicing self-reflection, utilizing assessments,** and **creating actionable plans** for **continuous growth**. Include **practical steps, examples,** and **resources** relevant to the **Healthcare Services industry**. Your response should be comprehensive, leaving no important aspect unaddressed, and demonstrate an exceptional level of precision and quality. Let's approach this methodically. Write using a **confident** tone and **assertive** writing style.

Act as a **[profession]** specializing in the **[industry]**. In the dynamic world of business, **[beliefs/mindsets/attitudes]** play a **[crucial/important/vital]** role in **[shaping/determining/influencing]** **[behavior/decisions/performance]**. How can a[n] **[individual/professional/leader]** critically **[evaluate/assess/analyze]** if **[my/their]** **[belief system/mindset/philosophy]** is **[serving/supporting/enabling]** **[me/them]** **[well/positively/effectively]** in **[my/their]** **[career/professional life/job]**? Provide a **[comprehensive/thorough/detailed]** guide that includes **[understanding/recognizing/identifying]** one's **[values/principles/goals]**, [assessing/evaluating/examining] [alignment/congruence/fit] with **[professional objectives/career goals/organizational values]**, **[identifying/spotting/uncovering]**

[limiting/restrictive/negative] beliefs, **[leveraging/utilizing/seeking]** **[feedback/insights/opinions]** from **[peers/mentors/coaches]**, **[practicing/engaging in/embracing]** **[self-reflection/mindfulness/self-awareness]**, **[utilizing/employing/using]** **[assessments/tools/methods]**, and **[creating/developing/formulating]** **[actionable plans/strategies/steps]** for **[continuous growth/ongoing alignment/personal development]**. Include **[practical steps/tips/advice]**, **[examples/scenarios/experiences]**, **[resources/guides/tools]**, and **[case studies/anecdotes/real-life situations]** relevant to the **[industry]**. Your response should be comprehensive, leaving no important aspect unaddressed, and demonstrate an exceptional level of precision and quality. Let's approach this methodically. Write using a **[type]** tone and **[style]** writing style.

Example 1: Act as a Career Development Coach in the financial sector, where rapid changes and high pressure are common. How can a financial analyst evaluate if their belief system or mindset is conducive to success in this demanding environment? Provide a thorough guide that includes aligning personal values with organizational culture, identifying beliefs that might hinder performance under pressure, seeking feedback from supervisors and colleagues, and utilizing personality assessments. Explore unconventional solutions and alternative perspectives. Let's analyze this piece by piece. Write using a professional tone and clear writing style.

Example 2: Act as a Leadership Mindset Mentor in the entrepreneurial ecosystem, where flexibility and resilience are key. How can a startup founder critically assess if their mindset aligns with the unpredictable nature of entrepreneurship? Provide a comprehensive examination that includes embracing a growth mindset, challenging preconceived notions about failure, leveraging mentorship and networking, and engaging in reflective journaling. Include actionable strategies, tools tailored for entrepreneurs, and real-life case studies. Discover rare insights and pioneering ideas. Let's dissect this carefully. Write using an informative tone and factual writing style.

PROMPT No 59

Growth-Mindset - Resilience - Learning

To provide team leaders, managers, and executives with a multi-faceted toolkit for instigating a shift from a fixed to a growth mindset within their teams. This transformation is pivotal for fostering resilience, encouraging continuous learning, and ultimately driving high performance.

Act as a **Mindset Transformation Consultant** specializing in **neuro-linguistic programming (NLP)** for the **e-commerce industry**. Could you delineate a comprehensive strategy to help me facilitate a shift from a fixed to a growth mindset within my team? I'd like insights into **the psychological principles that can be leveraged, effective messaging strategies, and daily practices that can induce this mindset shift**. Please provide **actionable steps** to induce this mindset shift. Additionally, outline potential pitfalls and how to avoid them. Let's dissect this systematically. Write using a **strategic** tone and an **analytical** writing style.

Act as a **[profession]** specializing in topic/specialization] for the **[industry]**. Could you delineate a comprehensive strategy to help me facilitate a shift from a fixed to a growth mindset within my team? I'd like insights into **[psychological principles, messaging strategies, daily practices]**. Please provide **[actionable steps/workshop ideas/team activities/KPIs]** to induce this mindset shift. Additionally, outline potential pitfalls and how to avoid them. Let's dissect this systematically. Write using a **[type]** tone and **[style]** writing style.

Example 1: Act as an Employee Development Specialist specializing in organizational behavior for the automotive industry. Could you help me develop an actionable plan for transforming my engineering team's fixed mindset into a growth mindset? I am particularly interested in applying behavioral psychology and team dynamics to this transformation. Offer practical steps, including sample dialogue for one-on-one sessions, training modules, and weekly challenges to foster this change. Also, specify common mistakes and recommended mitigation strategies. Let's examine this meticulously. Write using a targeted tone and a precise writing style.

Example 2: Act as a Leadership Coach specializing in cultural change management for the non-profit sector. Could you guide me in transitioning my administrative team from a fixed mindset to a growth mindset? I aim to leverage both internal and external communication channels to achieve this. Please provide a roadmap, complete with staff surveys, regular feedback mechanisms, and community-building exercises. Don't forget to highlight pitfalls such as cognitive biases and how to circumvent them. Let's explore this methodically. Write using a balanced tone and a comprehensive writing style.

PROMPT No 60

Self-Awareness - Performance - Optimization

To equip leaders with a holistic approach for facilitating conversations that help team members articulate their professional identities at their best. This involves not only defining what 'best' means but also recognizing the conditions that enable each individual to thrive. The goal is to boost self-awareness within the team, promote psychological safety, and identify ways to optimize work conditions for peak performance.

Act as a **Leadership Development Consultant** specializing in **Self-Awareness and Peak Performance** for the **automotive transportation industry**. Could you provide a **thorough guide** on how **to initiate and navigate conversations with my team members about who they are professionally when they're performing at their best**? I am particularly interested in **creating an environment that encourages self-exploration and open dialogue**. Include **specific question prompts, potential follow-up questions, and recommendations for facilitating a non-judgmental and constructive discussion** and organize the guide into **key sections such as preparation, engagement, and action steps**. Investigate unexpected avenues and creative pathways. Let's piece-by-piece analyze this matter. Write using a **constructive** tone and **solution-focused** writing style.

Act as a **[profession]** specializing in **[expertise/topic]** for the **[industry]**. Could you provide a **[comprehensive guide/list/resource]** on how to **[specific challenge/opportunity]**? I am particularly interested in **[focus areas/techniques]**. Include **[questions/prompts/examples]** and organize the guide into **[sections/stages]**. Investigate unexpected avenues and creative pathways. Let's piece-by-piece analyze this matter. Write using a **[type]** tone and **[style]** writing style.

Examples

Example 1: Act as a Performance Coach focusing on Individual Development. Could you create a step-by-step guide for me to discuss with my sales team about who they are professionally when they feel they're achieving their best results? I want to focus specifically on identifying the skills and mindsets that contribute to their success. Please provide a set of conversation prompts and potential activities that could augment this discussion. Separate the guide into sections such as pre-meeting prep, the main dialogue, and next steps. Suggest fresh approaches and inventive strategies. Let's carefully evaluate each segment. Write using a cautious tone and risk-averse writing style.

Example 2: Act as a Business Psychologist specializing in Self-Concept and Career Growth. Could you offer an in-depth manual on how to lead a reflective discussion with my product development team about who they are at their professional best? I'm keen on incorporating personality assessment tools and well-being metrics into the discussion. Include tips on how to interpret the data to foster a more productive work environment. Break the manual into segments like context-setting, data collection, interpretation, and actionable insights. Discover rare insights and pioneering ideas. Let's break this down into its constituent parts. Write using a critical tone and evaluative writing style.

PROMPT No 61

Tags

Purpose - Engagement - Mission

Goal

To provide leaders with a comprehensive strategy for facilitating discussions with team members about the underlying purpose served when striving to achieve company goals. These conversations aim to deepen team members' connection to their work by aligning individual values and motivations with the organizational mission, thereby enhancing engagement and performance.

Prompt

Act as a **Transformational Leadership Coach** specializing in **Purpose-Driven Organizations** for the **investment banking industry**. Could you offer a **comprehensive guide** on how to **initiate and manage a conversation with my team concerning the deeper purpose they are serving when working towards company objectives**? I'm particularly interested in **methods that help team members align their personal values with the corporate mission**. Include **varied question prompts, storytelling techniques, and, if applicable, software tools designed to map values to objectives**. Divide the guide into **segments such as the preparatory phase, conversation initiation, in-depth discussions, and post-conversation follow-up**. Examine overlooked possibilities and imaginative routes. Let's think about this step by step. Write using an engaging tone and interactive writing style.

Formula

Act as a **[profession]** specializing in **[specific area of focus]** for the **[industry]**. Could you offer a **[comprehensive guide/method]** on how to **[specific challenge/opportunity]**? I'm particularly interested in **[specific techniques/focus areas]**. Include **[interactive activities/questions/tools]**. Divide the guide into **[sections/phases/dialogue initiation/deep discussions]**. Examine overlooked possibilities and imaginative routes. Let's think about this step by step. Write using a **[type]** tone and **[style]** writing style.

Example 1: Act as a Corporate Culture Consultant focusing on Employee Engagement. Could you provide a complete guide on how to conduct a conversation with my sales team about the purpose behind their roles and how it aligns with the company's broader vision? I would like to use emotional intelligence models to encourage genuine sharing. Include thought-provoking question prompts, role-reversal exercises, and guided visualization techniques. Please partition the guide into the following phases: setting the context, initiating the conversation, fostering deep reflection, and crafting an action plan. Uncover scarce wisdom and trailblazing concepts. Let's scrutinize each segment with precision. Write using a creative tone and imaginative writing style.

Example 2: Act as a Professional Development Coach with a specialization in Organizational Behavior. Could you offer a guide for facilitating discussions within my R&D team on how their innovative projects serve the larger mission and vision of the company? I'm particularly keen on using self-assessment tools that can clarify value alignments between individual roles and company goals. Include a mix of open-ended questions, personality assessments, and peer feedback activities. Organize the guide into pre-discussion preparation, opening dialogue, core conversation, and next steps for follow-through. Furnish exceptional counsel and offbeat perspectives. Let's sequence our approach for clarity. Write using a value-centric tone and principles-guided writing style.

OPTIONS

PROMPT No 62

Decision-Making - Analysis - Strategy

To assist teams in critically evaluating and weighing the options available to them at work. This process will guide them in making informed decisions that align with their objectives and the overall mission of the company.

Act as a **Decision-Making Strategist** specializing in the **higher education industry**. Could you describe **an array of techniques that my team could consider to carefully analyze the pros and cons of the different options they currently have at their work**? This is essential in **facilitating better decisions that align with our strategic goals**. Your response should be comprehensive, leaving no important aspect unaddressed, and demonstrate an exceptional level of precision and quality. Let's consider each facet of this topic. Write using an **informative** tone and **analytical** writing style.

Act as a **[profession]** specializing in **[industry]**. Could you describe **[contextual challenge/opportunity]**? This is essential in **[desired outcome]**. Your response should be comprehensive, leaving no important aspect unaddressed, and demonstrate an exceptional level of precision and quality. Let's consider each facet of this topic. Write using a **[type]** tone and **[style]** writing style.

Example 1: Act as a Strategic Decision-making Coach specializing in the technology sector. Could you detail the techniques that my software development team could consider to meticulously evaluate the pros and cons of different software frameworks and methodologies? This is essential in selecting the best approach for our projects, aligned with our innovation goals. Let's break down both conventional wisdom and cutting-edge practices. Write using an engaging tone and methodical writing style.

Example 2: Act as an Organizational Analyst specializing in healthcare. Could you elucidate the various strategies that my medical team could consider to weigh the benefits and drawbacks of different treatment options for patients? This is essential in providing optimal patient care and aligning with medical ethics. Let's explore this with both evidence-based methods and patient-centered considerations. Write using a compassionate tone and evidence-based writing style.

PROMPT No 63

Appreciation - Feedback - Listening

To provide leaders with a structured approach for effectively discussing the positive aspects of a work experience or project with their team. This aims to foster a culture of appreciation, constructive feedback, and continuous improvement.

Act as a **Leadership Communication Specialist** specializing in the **automotive industry**. Could you **outline** the **best practices** for discussing what **went right** in a **recent work experience or project** with **my** team? Include **frameworks** for **positive feedback, techniques for active listening, and methods for encouraging team dialogue**. Let's sequentially address each element. Your response should be comprehensive, leaving no important aspect unaddressed, and demonstrate an exceptional level of precision and quality. Write using a **constructive** tone and a **facilitative** writing style.

Act as a **[profession]** specializing in the **[industry]**. Could you **[outline/describe/explain]** the **[best practices/guidelines/methodologies]** for discussing what **[went right/succeeded/excelled]** in a **[recent/past/current]** **[work experience/project/assignment]** with **[my/our/the]** team? Include **[frameworks/techniques/methods]** for **[positive feedback/active listening/team dialogue]**. Let's sequentially address each element. Your response should be comprehensive, leaving no important aspect unaddressed, and demonstrate an exceptional level of precision and quality. Write using a **[type]** tone and **[style]** writing style.

Example 1: Act as a Team Building Coach specializing in the tech industry. Could you describe the guidelines for discussing what succeeded in a recent software development project with my engineering team? Include the "Start-Stop-Continue" framework, empathetic listening techniques, and methods for fostering open dialogue. Let's tackle this in a phased manner. Write using an empathetic tone and an engaging writing style. Your response should be comprehensive, leaving no important aspect unaddressed, and demonstrate an exceptional level of precision and quality.

Example 2: Act as an Organizational Development Consultant specializing in the finance sector. Could you explain the methodologies for discussing what excelled in a past financial audit with our accounting team? Include the "Appreciative Inquiry" framework, active listening techniques, and Socratic questioning methods. Let's deconstruct this subject stepwise. Write using a motivational tone and an inspirational writing style. Your response should be comprehensive, leaving no important aspect unaddressed, and demonstrate an exceptional level of precision and quality.

PROMPT No 64

Organizational-Behavior - Empathy - Motivation

To enable team leaders and managers to understand the underlying factors and motivations that influence their team members' choices at work. This understanding will lead to more effective management, improved communication, and the ability to align team choices with organizational goals and values.

Act as an **Organizational Behavior Specialist** specializing in the **retail industry**. Could you guide me through the process of identifying and understanding **the factors that have influenced my team members' choices at work**? This includes considering **individual motivations, environmental influences, organizational culture, and other underlying elements**. Gaining this understanding is crucial for **more targeted coaching, better decision-making, and fostering a culture of empathy and alignment**. Please provide a comprehensive and insightful approach, considering various **psychological theories, assessment tools, and practical strategies**. Let's analyze this piece by piece. Write using an **instructive** tone and **analytical** writing style.

Act as a **[profession]** specializing in the **[industry]**. Could you guide me through the process of identifying and understanding **[contextual challenge/opportunity]?** This includes considering **[specific factors or elements]**. Gaining this understanding is crucial for **[desired outcome]**. Please provide a comprehensive and insightful approach, considering various **[methods, theories, or tools]**. Let's analyze this piece by piece. Write using a **[type]** tone and **[style]** writing style.

Example 1: Act as a Human Resources Consultant specializing in the manufacturing industry. Could you help me discern the factors that are affecting the choices and decision-making of my production team? This includes examining personal values, team dynamics, leadership styles, and workplace environment. Grasping these influences is key to improving collaboration, enhancing productivity, and building a more cohesive team culture. Please outline a systematic and insightful method, exploring various behavioral theories, surveys, interviews, and observation techniques. Let's dissect this carefully. Write using a professional tone and engaging writing style.

Example 2: Act as a Leadership Coach specializing in the non-profit sector. Could you assist me in uncovering the underlying motivations and factors that guide my team members' choices in our organization? This involves understanding personal passions, organizational mission alignment, peer influences, and leadership impact. Comprehending these aspects is vital for inspiring commitment, ensuring alignment with our goals, and nurturing a purpose-driven culture. Please offer a thorough and empathetic approach, encompassing motivational theories, reflective exercises, group workshops, and continuous feedback mechanisms. Let's take this one step at a time. Write using a compassionate tone and constructive writing style.

PERFORMANCE

PROMPT No 65

Recognition - Team-Dynamics - Tech

To equip leaders with a comprehensive guide on how to initiate and facilitate impactful discussions around the professional advancements team members have gained through their involvement in team projects or group tasks. The ultimate aim is to foster an environment of recognition, self-awareness, and enthusiasm for continuous improvement.

As a **Career Development Specialist** with a focus on **team dynamics** for the **tech industry**, could you guide me through **the process of holding a discussion with my team to reflect on how their participation in team projects has contributed to their professional growth**? Please include **techniques for starting the conversation, types of questions to ask for in-depth reflection, and strategies to encourage an open exchange of ideas**. Ensure the guide covers **how to recognize individual and collective accomplishments and how to channel this recognition into future team and personal development goals**. Introduce innovative perspectives and emerging trends. Let's go through this methodically. Write using an informative tone and factual writing style.

As a [profession] with a focus on **[topic]** for the **[industry]**, could you guide me through **[contextual challenge/opportunity]**? Please include **[methods/techniques]**. Ensure the guide covers **[aspects/topics to be addressed]**. Introduce innovative perspectives and emerging trends. Let's go through this methodically. Write using a **[type]** tone and **[style]** writing style.

Example 1: As a Performance Coach specializing in career progression in the legal industry, could you help me discuss with my team how their efforts on recent case collaborations have advanced their professional skills? Include conversation starters, reflective questions that explore skill development, and methodologies to encourage open dialog. Make sure the guide elaborates on recognizing milestone achievements and the utility of this recognition for future growth prospects. Offer avant-garde viewpoints like gamification of milestones. Let's break this down piece by piece. Write using an uplifting tone and an inspiring writing style.

Example 2: As an Organizational Psychologist with a focus on motivation in the non-profit sector, could you assist me in conducting a conversation with my team about the professional gains they've made through recent community projects? Include methods for initiating the discussion, probing questions that encourage thoughtful introspection, and actionable steps for celebrating and leveraging these gains for future projects. Ensure the guide discusses the psychological benefits of recognition and how they translate into higher engagement levels. Uncover unique angles such as leveraging storytelling for emotional engagement. Let's navigate this sequentially. Write using an empathetic tone and a supportive writing style.

PROMPT No 66

Tags

Obstacles - Self-Improvement - Introspection

Goal

To assist individuals, particularly leaders and professionals, in identifying personal barriers that might be hindering their growth or ability to reach their full potential, and guide them through the initial steps they can take to overcome these obstacles. The ultimate aim is to promote self-awareness, personal development, and effective strategies for self-improvement.

Prompt

Act as a **Personal Development Coach** specializing in **self-awareness and growth strategies** for the **professional services industry**. Could you elucidate the **techniques to recognize what might be obstructing me from realizing my fullest potential**? What are the **initial critical steps I can undertake to cope with these impediments**? Respond separately to each question. Include both **introspective methodologies and practical exercises, considering various personal dynamics, professional contexts, and life stages**. Provide **tailored insights and actionable advice**. Let's unravel this progressively. Write using a **compassionate** tone and an **inspiring** writing style.

Formula

Act as a **[profession]** specializing in **[specific focus]** for the **[industry]**. Could you elucidate the **[contextual challenge/opportunity]**? What are the **[specific requirements]**? Respond separately to each question. Include both **[additional specifications]**. Provide **[desired outcome]**. Let's unravel this progressively. Write using a **[type]** tone and **[style]** writing style.

Examples

Example 1: Act as a Career Mentor specializing in overcoming professional roadblocks for the mining industry. Could you explain how to identify the barriers that might be preventing me from excelling in my career? What are the initial steps and reflections I should engage in? Respond separately to each question. Include both self-assessment tools and professional development activities. Provide insightful analysis and a personalized growth plan, considering various career stages, industries, and personal attributes. Let's explore this methodically. Write using a constructive tone and a motivational writing style.

Example 2: Act as a Life Coach specializing in personal growth and self-discovery for the defense industry. Could you guide me through the process of recognizing what might be hindering me from achieving personal success and happiness? What are the initial vital practices and mental exercises I can adopt? Respond separately to each question. Include both psychological assessments and mindfulness techniques. Provide holistic guidance and emotional support, considering various life circumstances, personal values, and individual needs. Let's approach this empathetically. Write using a nurturing tone and an empowering writing style.

PROMPT No 67

Tags

Benefits - Organizational-Psychology - Tech

Goal

To help team leaders, managers, and executives accurately identify the primary benefits their team members have derived from working at their company. This understanding will enable them to refine their leadership approach, improve team morale, and optimize talent retention strategies.

Prompt

As an **professional coach** with a focus on **organizational psychology and team dynamics** for **the tech industry.** Could you guide me through a comprehensive method to **find out what my team members consider to be the most beneficial aspects of working in our organization**? This method should include **designing an evaluation framework, choosing the most appropriate tools for data collection (e.g., surveys, interviews, etc.), and analyzing the gathered information to derive actionable insights**. Make sure to address potential biases and ethical considerations, providing examples and templates for each stage of the process. Explore unconventional solutions and alternative perspectives. Let's take this one step at a time. Write using a **formal** tone and **concise** writing style.

Formula

Act as a **[profession]** with a focus on **[specific area of expertise]** for the **[industry]**. Could you guide me through a comprehensive method to **[specific task or objective]?** This method should include **[list of detailed components]**. Make sure to address potential biases and ethical considerations, providing examples and templates for each stage of the process. Explore unconventional solutions and alternative perspectives. Let's take this one step at a time. Write using a **[type]** tone and **[style]** writing style.

Examples

Example 1: Act as an expert HR Consultant with a focus on employee engagement for the . Could you guide me through a comprehensive method to assess what factors contribute the most to job satisfaction among my team members? Include designing a structured survey, selecting the right distribution channels, and employing statistical methods to analyze the data. Address potential biases like recency and selection bias, providing sample questions and calculation models for each stage of the process. Unearth hidden gems and non-traditional methods. Let's go through this systematically. Write using a strategic tone and forward-thinking writing style.

Example 2: Act as an expert Team Coach with a specialization in talent management. Could you guide me through a comprehensive method to find out what my team members believe are the most critical skill sets they've developed while working in our organization? This should include constructing a detailed interview guide, selecting suitable interviewees from different hierarchies and departments, and employing qualitative analysis methods for insights extraction. Address ethical considerations like confidentiality and data handling, providing sample questions and a data analysis template for each stage of the process. Provide an exhaustive and all-encompassing analysis. Let's think about this step by step. Write using an engaging tone and interactive writing style.

PROMPT No 68

Tags

CognitivePsychology - Behavioral - DecisionMaking

Goal

To help team leaders, managers, and executives understand the cognitive and emotional factors that influence what their team members choose to focus on in the workplace. By doing so, leaders can better allocate resources, tailor communication strategies, and improve productivity.

Prompt

As an **organizational psychology coach** expert in **cognitive psychology and team dynamics** for the **publishing industry**. Could you provide me with a structured approach to **understand what influences my team's decision on what to pay attention to during work**? This should include **how to formulate targeted questions or observations, select appropriate tools for data collection such as behavioral analysis or surveys, and a method to synthesize and apply these insights in a meaningful way**. Also, please outline potential biases and ethical considerations to be aware of in this process. Explore unconventional solutions and alternative perspectives. Let's think about this step by step. Write using a **formal** tone and **concise** writing style.

Formula

Act as **[profession]** expert in **[specific area of expertise]** for the **[industry]**. Could you provide me with a structured approach to **[specific task or objective]**? This should include **[list of detailed components]**. Also, please outline **[potential challenges and limitations]** to be aware of in this process. Explore unconventional solutions and alternative perspectives. Let's think about this step by step. Write using a **[type]** tone and **[style]** writing style.

Examples

Example 1: Act as an expert Organizational Psychologist with a focus on team dynamics for the retail industry. Could you provide me with a structured approach to analyze what factors contribute most to my team members' decision on what tasks to prioritize? This should include creating behavioral markers to observe, choosing between direct observation and anonymous surveys, and synthesizing this information to improve our project management approach. Also, please outline biases like confirmation and observer bias, providing mitigation strategies for each. Unearth hidden gems and non-traditional methods. Let's proceed by examining each component. Write using a motivational tone and inspiring writing style.

Example 2: Act as an expert Leadership Coach with a specialization in cognitive behavior for the e-commerce industry. Could you provide me with a structured approach to discover what influences my team's decision on which meetings and communications they consider most valuable? This should include formulating targeted questions that probe their decision-making, selecting the most appropriate method for gathering this information such as one-on-one interviews or group discussions, and synthesizing these insights to refine our internal communication strategies. Also, please outline potential ethical considerations like confidentiality and informed consent, offering guidelines on how to navigate them. Offer extraordinary advice and non-mainstream opinions. Let's delineate the facets one by one. Write using a strategic tone and forward-thinking writing style.

PRIORITIES

PROMPT No 69

TimeManagement - Strategies - Priorities

To furnish business leaders, managers, and team members with a broad spectrum of strategies to manage multiple key priorities simultaneously. This includes traditional and innovative approaches, practical tools, and customized insights that can be implemented across various industries, organizational structures, and team dynamics.

Act as a **Time Management Specialist** specializing in **corporate productivity** for the **natural resources industry**. Could you provide **a comprehensive examination of various strategies, tools, and methodologies for managing multiple key priorities all at once**? This includes **a mix of time-tested techniques, novel approaches, potential pitfalls, and ways to integrate these strategies into daily workflow**. Provide **unique insights and overlooked opportunities**, considering various **industry norms, organizational hierarchies, and team sizes**. Let's dissect this progressively. Write using an **instructive** tone and **analytical** writing style.

Act as a **[profession]** specializing in **[specific focus]** for the **[industry]**. Could you provide **[contextual challenge/opportunity]?** This includes **[specific requirements]**. Provide **[desired outcome]**, considering various **[additional specifications]**. Let's dissect this progressively. Write using a **[type]** tone and **[style]** writing style.

Example 1: Act as a Productivity Coach specializing in the healthcare industry. Could you present a thorough exploration of methods for healthcare professionals to manage numerous critical tasks simultaneously? This includes various scheduling techniques, technology tools, team collaboration strategies, and alignment with patient care standards. Provide actionable steps, unique cases, and potential challenges, considering different healthcare settings, professional roles, and regulatory environments. Let's analyze this systematically. Write using a clear tone and a methodical writing style.

Example 2: Act as an Organizational Efficiency Expert specializing in technology startups. Could you delineate strategies that tech teams can employ to juggle multiple product development priorities at once? This includes agile methodologies, priority-setting frameworks, collaboration tools, and alignment with rapid innovation cycles. Provide hands-on recommendations, pioneering concepts, and industry-specific insights, considering different development stages, team structures, and market demands. Let's explore this in a step-by-step manner. Write using an engaging tone and a practical writing style.

PROMPT No 70

To gain insights on specific strategies or techniques to effectively determine the genuine wants and desires of team members, enhancing team management and satisfaction.

Team-Management - Empathy - Satisfaction

Given the importance of **understanding the genuine wants and desires of team members**, as an **Executive Coach** and in an **empathetic and open-minded tone**, could you suggest specific strategies or techniques I can utilize for **this purpose**?

Given the importance of **[contextual challenge/opportunity]**, as a **[profession]** and in a **[tone of voice]**, could you suggest specific strategies or techniques **[I/Name/Role]** can utilize for **[desired outcome]**?

Example 1: Given the importance of understanding the genuine wants and desires of healthcare staff, as a Leadership Development Consultant and in a respectful and patient tone, could you suggest specific strategies or techniques a healthcare manager can utilize for this purpose?

Example 2: As a Team Coach, in a supportive and considerate tone, could you suggest specific strategies or techniques I can utilize to effectively determine the genuine wants and desires of my engineering team members? This advice is particularly relevant given the importance of employee satisfaction in retaining top talent.

PROGRESS

PROMPT No 71

Inspiration - Alignment - Potential

To guide you in facilitating conversations with your team about the possibilities and potential outcomes when members are performing at their best, thereby fostering motivation, alignment with goals, and collective achievement.

Act as a **Leadership Communication Specialist** specializing in the **financial services industry**. Could you provide me with **insights, strategies, and techniques on how I can be better prepared to have conversations with my team about the possibilities when they are performing at their best**? The ultimate goal is to **inspire them to reach their full potential, align with organizational values, and contribute positively to the team's success**. Share distinctive methods, role-playing scenarios, and communication tips, considering different team dynamics, performance levels, and individual aspirations. Let's dissect this carefully. Write using an **inspirational** tone and **engaging** writing style.

Act as a **[profession]** specializing in the **[industry]**. Could you provide me with **[contextual challenge/opportunity]**? The ultimate goal is to **[explicit desired outcome]**. Share distinctive methods, role-playing scenarios, and communication tips, considering different team dynamics, performance levels, and individual aspirations. Let's dissect this carefully. Write using a **[type]** tone and **[style]** writing style.

Examples

Example 1: Act as a Team Performance Coach specializing in the software development industry. Could you provide me with a comprehensive guide on having conversations with my development team about what the possibilities are when they excel? The ultimate goal is to foster innovation, promote collaboration, and drive project success. Share unique coaching methods, constructive feedback techniques, and cultural insights, considering various technical expertise, team collaboration, and project challenges. Let's analyze this piece by piece. Write using a constructive tone and analytical writing style.

Example 2: Act as an Organizational Development Consultant specializing in the non-profit sector. Could you provide me with in-depth strategies for engaging my team in conversations about their highest potential and the positive impacts they can make? The ultimate goal is to empower them to make significant contributions to our mission and the communities we serve. Share thought-provoking questions, empathy-driven approaches, and community-centered examples, considering various social causes, team motivations, and organizational missions. Let's take this one step at a time. Write using a compassionate tone and motivational writing style.

PROMPT No 72

Tags

Satisfaction - Evaluation - Motivation

Goal

To understand and evaluate the level of satisfaction within a team regarding the pace of their progress in a specific industry, with the aim of identifying areas of alignment or discontent to enhance motivation, satisfaction, and performance.

Prompt

Act as a **Team Development Specialist** specializing in the **e-commerce industry**. Could you guide me through **a detailed process to evaluate the level of satisfaction of my team regarding the pace of their progress**? This is particularly vital in recognizing areas of contentment or concern and devising strategies tailored to our industry. Please provide a meticulous and wide-ranging response, including methods, tools, or strategies unique to our sector. Let's think about this step by step. Write using an **analytical** tone and **constructive** writing style.

Formula

Act as a **[profession]** specializing in the **[industry]**. Could you guide me through **[contextual challenge/opportunity]**? This is particularly vital in **[desired outcome]**. Please provide a meticulous and wide-ranging response, including methods, tools, or strategies unique to our sector. Let's think about this step by step. Write using a **[type]** tone and **[style]** writing style.

Examples

Example 1: Act as an Employee Engagement Consultant specializing in the tech industry. Could you guide me through the process to evaluate the satisfaction level of my software development team regarding their project progress? Share distinctive guidance and unexplored options in your response. Let's dissect this carefully. Write using a polite tone and assertive writing style.

Example 2: Act as a Leadership Trainer specializing in the insurance industry. Could you guide me through the methods to assess the satisfaction level of my sales team regarding their growth and achievements? Your response should be comprehensive, leaving no important aspect unaddressed, and demonstrate an exceptional level of precision and quality in the context of the insurance sector. Let's analyze this piece by piece. Write using a motivated tone and conversational writing style.

PURPOSE

PROMPT No 73

Consciousness - Alignment - Leadership

To gain specific steps and techniques that can be adopted to successfully improve a team's understanding and consciousness of their goals and objectives.

As a **Leadership Development Consultant**, adopting an **encouraging and supportive tone**, could you provide specific steps and techniques that **I** can adopt to successfully improve **my team**'s understanding and consciousness of their **goals and objectives**? This is particularly relevant given the goal of **enhancing their alignment with the organization's mission and vision**.

As a **[profession]**, adopting a **[tone of voice]**, could you provide specific steps and techniques that **[I/Name/Role]** can adopt to successfully improve **[my/their]** **[team/group/department]**'s understanding and consciousness of their **[contextual challenge/opportunity]**? This is particularly relevant given the goal of **[desired outcome]**.

Example 1: Adopting an enthusiastic and optimistic tone, as a Team Coach, could you provide specific steps and techniques that I can adopt to successfully improve my project team's understanding and consciousness of their project objectives? This is particularly relevant given the goal of enhancing their alignment with the project's mission and vision.
Example 2: As a Human Resources (HR) Consultant, adopting a clear and concise tone, could you provide specific steps and techniques that a department head can adopt to successfully improve their faculty's understanding and consciousness of their academic goals? This is particularly relevant given the goal of enhancing their alignment with the institution's mission and vision.

PROMPT No 74

Metrics - Criteria - Quantitative

To provide leaders with a robust framework for identifying and measuring the criteria or indicators that signify the successful achievement of their intentions or objectives. The focus is on creating actionable, quantifiable metrics that align with both individual and organizational goals.

Act as a **Performance Metrics Analyst** specializing in the **finance industry**. Could you **delineate** the **criteria** that will **signify** the **achievement** of my **intention** in a **strategic project**? Include **both qualitative and quantitative metrics, and discuss how these align with broader organizational KPIs**. Let's sequentially address each element. Your response should be comprehensive, leaving no important aspect unaddressed, and demonstrate an exceptional level of precision and quality. Write using an **analytical** tone and a **data-driven** writing style.

Act as a **[profession]** specializing in the **[industry]**. Could you **[delineate/elucidate/outline]** the **[criteria/indicators/metrics]** that will **[signify/indicate/mark]** the **[achievement/success/completion]** of my **[intention/objective/goal]** in **[context, e.g., a strategic project/business initiative]**? Include **[both/and/or]** **[qualitative/quantitative]** **[metrics/indicators]**, and discuss how these **[align/integrate/correlate]** with **[broader/wider/organizational]** **[KPIs/objectives/goals]**. Let's sequentially address each element. Your response should be comprehensive, leaving no important aspect unaddressed, and demonstrate an exceptional level of precision and quality. Write using a **[type]** tone and **[style]** writing style.

Example 1: Act as a Business Intelligence Consultant specializing in the healthcare industry. Could you outline the criteria that will signify the achievement of my intention in improving patient satisfaction? Include both qualitative metrics like patient feedback and quantitative metrics like readmission rates, and discuss how these align with our hospital's KPIs. Let's methodically dissect each component. Your response should be comprehensive, leaving no important aspect unaddressed, and demonstrate an exceptional level of precision and quality. Write using a diagnostic tone and an evidence-based writing style.

Example 2: Act as a Leadership Coach specializing in the tech industry. Could you elucidate the indicators that will mark the success of my intention in fostering a culture of innovation? Include both qualitative indicators like employee engagement surveys and quantitative indicators like the number of new patents filed, and discuss how these integrate with our company's strategic objectives. Let's carefully evaluate each segment. Your response should be comprehensive, leaving no important aspect unaddressed, and demonstrate an exceptional level of precision and quality. Write using a diagnostic tone and an evidence-based writing style.

PROMPT No 75

Interpersonal - Inquiry - Non-Verbal

To empower business leaders, mentors, and coaches to engage in deeper one-on-one conversations with their colleagues. This aims to subtly identify their unexpressed desires or aspirations, which may be crucial for enhancing job satisfaction, team dynamics, and overall productivity.

Act as a **corporate communications expert** with a focus on **interpersonal skills** in the **healthcare industry**. Can you provide me with **nuanced strategies** for understanding **my colleague desires or aspires to achieve without directly asking them during a**

one-on-one discussion? Please incorporate **non-verbal cues, open-ended questions, and indirect methods of inquiry**. Make sure to cover how to **interpret the information gained and how to utilize it effectively**. Navigate through unexplored realms and revolutionary paradigms. Let's sequentially address each element. Write using a **friendly** tone and **approachable** writing style.

Act as a **[profession]** with a specialization in **[area of expertise]** in the **[specific industry]**. Could you provide me with **[strategy/framework/method]** for understanding **[challenge or topic]?** Please incorporate **[tools/techniques/areas to focus on]**. Make sure to cover how to **[actions or objectives to meet]**. Navigate through unexplored realms and revolutionary paradigms. Let's sequentially address each element. Write using a **[type]** tone and **[style]** writing style.

Example 1: Act as an organizational behaviorist with a specialization in employee motivation in the finance industry. Could you guide me through tactics to identify unspoken goals or aspirations my colleague may have, during our one-on-one meeting? Please include techniques like active listening, the Socratic method, and reading body language. Make sure to explain how this understanding can contribute to a more cohesive work environment. Investigate unexpected avenues and creative pathways for employee retention. Let's tackle this in a phased manner. Maintain an encouraging tone and provide specific examples.

Example 2: Act as an HR consultant with a specialization in employee engagement for the marketing industry. Can you share approaches to subtly determine what my colleague might be aspiring to, without explicitly asking during our one-on-one discussions? Include advice on empathetic questioning, mirroring techniques, and behavioral observations. Make sure to address how this knowledge can improve team dynamics and employee satisfaction. Delve into uncharted territories and groundbreaking concepts to create an authentic connection. Let's methodically dissect each component. Use a respectful tone and a how-to approach.

PROMPT No 76

Cohesion - Purpose - Reflection

To acquire a comprehensive, actionable guide on methods for reflecting with a team on the deeper understanding they have gained about their collective purpose, with the aim of enhancing team cohesion, individual motivation, and overall organizational alignment.

As a **Purpose-Driven Leadership Coach** in the **non-profit industry**, could you provide an exhaustive guide outlining the methods **my team and I** can employ to reflect on the deeper understanding we have all gained about our **purpose**? Please include **both individual reflection exercises and group activities**. Break down your advice into specific sections, reinforcing each with **quantifiable metrics**. Explore unconventional approaches and diverse viewpoints. Let's dissect this carefully. Write using an **analytical** tone and a **structured** writing style.

As a **[profession]** in the **[industry]**, could you provide an exhaustive guide outlining the methods **[my team and I/Name/Role and their team]** can employ to reflect on the deeper understanding we have all gained about our **[purpose/specific goal]**? Please include both

[individual reflection exercises/group activities]. Break down your advice into specific sections, reinforcing each with **[quantifiable metrics/scholarly literature].** Explore unconventional approaches and diverse viewpoints. Let's dissect this carefully. Write using a **[type]** tone and **[style]** writing style.

Example 1: As a Team Development Specialist in the technology industry, could you provide an exhaustive guide outlining the methods my engineering team and I can employ to reflect on the deeper understanding we have all gained about our purpose in developing sustainable technologies? Please include both journaling exercises and team-building workshops. Divide your insights into separate modules, each validated by empirical findings and authoritative sources. Investigate unexpected avenues and creative pathways. Let's examine each dimension meticulously. Write using a focused tone and a concise writing style.

Example 2: As an Organizational Psychologist in the education sector, could you provide an exhaustive guide outlining the methods my faculty and I can employ to reflect on the deeper understanding we have all gained about our educational mission? Please include both self-assessment tools and group discussions. Structure your guidance into individual components, each backed by statistical analysis and peer-reviewed studies. Unearth hidden gems and non-traditional methods. Let's tackle this in a phased manner. Write using a balanced tone and a nuanced writing style.

RELATIONSHIPS

PROMPT No 77

Trust - Assessment - Collaboration

To understand, foster, and implement strategies that enhance trust and open communication between your team and other departments within the organization, thereby leading to improved collaboration and increased productivity.

Act as an **organizational psychologist** with a specialization in **interpersonal dynamics** for the **healthcare sector**. Could you guide me through the **intricacies of fostering a culture that promotes open and trusting relationships between my team and other departments**? Please include **methodologies for assessing trust levels and actionable steps to improve them**. Make sure to cover how **the role of communication in trust-building, and the impact of trust on inter-departmental collaboration could be further developed**. Delve into uncharted territories and groundbreaking concepts to sustain this practice. Let's dissect this in a structured manner. Write using an **empathetic** tone and a **narrative** writing style.

Act as a **[profession]** with a specialization in **[area of expertise]** for the **[industry]**. Could you guide me through **[specific challenge/opportunity]**? Please include **[methods/techniques]**. Make sure to cover how **[key areas/topics]**. Delve into uncharted territories and groundbreaking concepts to sustain this practice. Let's dissect this in a structured manner. Write using a **[type]** tone and **[style]** writing style.

Example 1: Act as a corporate communications expert with a specialization in team dynamics for the software industry. Could you walk me through the best practices to improve trust and open dialogue between my team and the client-facing departments? Please share frameworks for assessing and scaling trust. Make sure to focus on the role of transparency and open-door policies. Navigate through unexplored realms and revolutionary paradigms to enhance team collaboration. Write with an analytical tone and an informative writing style.

Example 2: Act as an HR consultant with a specialization in conflict resolution for the retail sector. Can you help me formulate a plan to build more trusting and open relationships between my sales team and the logistics department? Include metrics for measuring trust and actionable interventions. Make sure to consider how to manage conflicts that might arise. Offer extraordinary advice and non-mainstream opinions to refine this practice. Write with a balanced tone and a formal writing style.

PROMPT No 78

Tags

Selection - Software - Team-building

Goal

To assist business leaders in effectively selecting the right team members for a project by considering technical knowledge, experience, and personality. The aim is to provide leaders with a comprehensive method to assess and match team members to project needs, thus enhancing the chances of project success.

Prompt

Act as an **Executive Coach** with a specialization in **talent management and team formation** for the **software industry**. Could you guide me through **the process of selecting the right people to work on a project based on their technical knowledge, experience, and personality**? Please include **assessment tools, interview questions, and team-building exercises**. Make sure to cover how **to evaluate the suitability of a team member based on these three factors**. Delve into uncharted territories and groundbreaking concepts to optimize team selection. Let's dissect this in a structured manner. Write using a **practical** tone and a **how-to** writing style.

Formula

Act as a **[profession]** with a specialization in **[area of expertise]** for the **[industry]**. Could you guide me through **[specific challenge/opportunity]**? Please include **[methods/techniques]**. Make sure to cover how **[key areas/topics]**. Delve into uncharted territories and groundbreaking concepts to optimize team selection. Let's dissect this in a structured manner. Write using a **[type]** tone and **[style]** writing style.

Examples

Example 1: Act as a Human Resources Consultant with a specialization in team dynamics for the retail industry, could you guide me through the selection process of forming a customer service team with a balance of technical skills and interpersonal abilities? Please include scoring systems, behavioral questions, and personality tests. Make sure to cover how to reconcile the results of these various assessments. Suggest fresh approaches and inventive strategies to form high-performing customer service teams. Let's dissect this in a structured manner. Write using an engaging tone and a conversational writing style.

Example 2: Act as an Organizational Behavior Specialist with a specialization in project management for the automotive industry, could you guide me through developing a framework for selecting engineers based on both their technical skills and their ability to work in a team? Please include evaluation matrices, skills assessment tests, and group dynamics exercises. Make sure to cover how to finalize the team based on these assessments. Offer extraordinary advice and non-mainstream opinions to maximize team efficiency. Let's dissect this in a structured manner. Write using an analytical tone and a data-driven writing style.

PROMPT No 79

Tags
Presence - Mindfulness - Contemplative

Goal
To develop a comprehensive and actionable strategy for identifying the factors that hinder one's ability to be fully present. The aim is to provide a roadmap for self-awareness and improvement, supported by evidence-based methods and practices

Prompt
As a **Mindfulness Consultant** in the **education sector**, could you delineate a **structured approach** to help **me** identify the factors that hinder **my** ability to be **fully present**? Include **actionable tactics** for **short-term** implementation. Organize your insights into **distinct themes**, each substantiated by **references from trustworthy studies**. Investigate unexpected avenues and creative pathways. Let's **examine each dimension meticulously**. Write using a **contemplative** tone and a **reflective** writing style.

Formula
As a **[profession]** in the **[industry]**, could you delineate a **[structured approach/comprehensive strategy/detailed plan]** to help **[me/us/them]** identify the factors that hinder **[my/our/their]** ability to be **[fully present/engaged/focused]**? Include **[actionable tactics/immediate steps/practical measures] for [immediate/short-term/long-term]** implementation. Organize your insights into **[distinct themes/clear categories/discrete units]**, each substantiated by **[references from/data from/evidence from] [trustworthy studies/credible research/authoritative publications]**. Investigate unexpected avenues and creative pathways. Let's **[examine each dimension meticulously/deconstruct this subject stepwise]**. Write using a **[contemplative/reflective/thoughtful]** tone and a **[reflective/insightful/nuanced]** writing style.

Examples

Example 1: As a Performance Coach in the technology industry, could you delineate a comprehensive strategy to help me identify the factors that hinder my ability to be fully present? Include practical measures for short-term implementation. Organize your insights into clear categories, each substantiated by data from credible research. Discover rare insights and pioneering ideas. Let's deconstruct this subject stepwise. Write using a contemplative tone and an insightful writing style.

Example 2: As a Life Coach in the healthcare sector, could you delineate a detailed plan to help me identify the factors that hinder my ability to be engaged? Include immediate steps for long-term implementation. Organize your insights into discrete units, each substantiated by evidence from authoritative publications. Explore unconventional solutions and alternative perspectives. Let's examine each dimension meticulously. Write using a reflective tone and a nuanced writing style.

PROMPT No 80

Resourcefulness - Strategy - Human Resources

To equip business leaders with robust tools and strategies for accurately determining the additional human resources needed to complete a project successfully. This will cover various aspects such as skill sets, time commitment, and budget considerations.

Act as a **Business Strategist** with a specialization in **project management and human resources** for the **technology sector**. Could you guide me through **the methodology of assessing the extra human resources needed to successfully execute a project**? Please include **metrics, evaluation criteria, and time management strategies**. Make sure to cover how **to balance the allocation of existing and new resources**. Delve into uncharted territories and groundbreaking concepts. Let's dissect this in a structured manner. Write using a **comprehensive** tone and a **how-to** writing style.

Act as a [profession] with a specialization in [area of expertise] for the [industry]. Could you guide me through [specific challenge/opportunity]? Please include [methods/techniques]. Make sure to cover how [key areas/topics]. Delve into uncharted territories and groundbreaking concepts. Let's dissect this in a structured manner. Write using a [type] tone and [style] writing style.

Example 1: Act as an Operations Manager with a specialization in workforce planning for the healthcare industry. Could you guide me through evaluating the need for additional nursing staff for an upcoming department expansion? Please include headcount metrics, workload assessments, and budget impact analysis. Make sure to cover how to coordinate existing staff with new hires. Investigate unexpected avenues and creative pathways to achieve optimal staffing levels. Let's dissect this in a structured manner. Write using an empathetic tone and an evidence-based writing style.

Example 2: Act as a Financial Analyst with a specialization in labor economics for the manufacturing sector. Could you guide me through determining the extra manpower needed to scale our production by 50% in the next quarter? Please include cost-to-company calculations, skill gap analyses, and shift planning. Make sure to cover how to mitigate the financial risks associated with the scaling. Navigate through unexplored realms and revolutionary paradigms to master workforce planning. Let's dissect this in a structured manner. Write using a data-driven tone and an analytical writing style.

PROMPT No 81

Relationships - Communication - Barriers

To provide entrepreneurs and business leaders a structured approach for initiating relationship enhancement with clients or colleagues, fostering improved communication and collaboration.

Act as a **Relationship Development Specialist** specializing in **Communication Skills** within the **corporate business sector**. Could you guide me through a **systematic and actionable approach to take the initial step in enhancing relationships with clients or colleagues**? Please include **identification of potential barriers, communication strategies, and key metrics to evaluate the effectiveness of the relationship enhancement initiatives**. Make sure to cover how **to maintain a constructive and professional demeanor during this process**. Explore **innovative and possibly unconventional solutions** to **foster a culture of open dialogue and continuous relationship improvement**. Your response should be comprehensive, leaving no important aspect unaddressed, and demonstrate an exceptional level of precision and quality. Let's think about this step by step. Write using a **professional** tone and a **methodical** writing style.

Act as a **[profession]** specializing in **[area of expertise]** within the **[industry]**. Could you guide me through **[specific challenge/opportunity]**? Please include **[methods/techniques]**. Make sure to cover how **[key areas/topics]**. Explore **[exploratory direction]** to **[desired outcome]**. Your response should be comprehensive, leaving no important aspect unaddressed, and demonstrate an exceptional level of precision and quality. Let's think about this step by step. Write using a **[type]** tone and a **[style]** writing style.

Example 1: Act as a Corporate Communication Advisor specializing in Emotional Intelligence within the technology sector. Could you guide me through the initial steps to foster stronger relationships with key stakeholders? Please include a diagnostic framework for assessing current relationship statuses, communication techniques for expressing commitment to enhancement, and metrics for tracking relationship progress. Make sure to cover how to handle any resistance or hesitation from stakeholders. Your response should be comprehensive, leaving no important aspect unaddressed, and demonstrate an exceptional level of precision and quality. Let's think about this step by step. Write using a solutions-oriented tone and a clear, instructional writing style.

Example 2: Act as a Team Building Consultant specializing in Conflict Resolution within the healthcare sector. Could you guide me through a structured approach for addressing concerns or issues raised by colleagues, as a stepping stone to improving inter-departmental relationships? Please include strategies for open dialogue, conflict resolution techniques, and mechanisms for ongoing feedback. Make sure to cover how to maintain a positive and constructive atmosphere during these discussions. Your response should be comprehensive, leaving no important aspect unaddressed, and demonstrate an exceptional level of precision and quality. Let's think about this step by step. Write using a balanced tone and a collaborative writing style.

PROMPT No 82

Tags

Motivation - Implementation - Satisfaction

Goal

To obtain a comprehensive, actionable framework that outlines methods for reflecting on the factors that fuel passion for work among team members. The aim is to enhance job satisfaction, improve team cohesion, and contribute to overall organizational success.

Prompt

As a **Motivational Strategist** in the **non-profit sector**, could you provide a **comprehensive strategy** detailing **methods** to help **me** and **my team** reflect on the factors that fuel **our** passion for work? Additionally, offer **actionable steps** for **immediate** implementation. Segment your insights into distinct modules, each supported by **evidence from reputable industry reports**. Investigate unexpected avenues and creative pathways. Let's **dissect this carefully**. Write using an **inspiring** tone and a **persuasive** writing style.

Formula

As a **[profession]** in the **[industry]**, could you provide a **[comprehensive strategy/thorough toolkit/detailed blueprint]** detailing the **[methods/techniques/approaches]** to help **[me/us/them]** reflect on the factors that fuel **[our/their/my]** passion for work? Additionally, offer **[actionable steps/initial measures/immediate tactics]** for **[immediate/short-term/long-term]** implementation. Segment your insights into distinct modules, each supported by **[evidence from/references from/data from]** **[reputable journals/credible research/authoritative publications/industry reports]**. Investigate unexpected avenues and creative pathways. Let's **[examine each dimension meticulously/dissect this carefully]**. Write using a **[inspiring/energizing/motivating]** tone and a **[persuasive/engaging/innovative]** writing style.

Examples

Example 1: As an Employee Engagement Consultant in the healthcare sector, could you provide a detailed blueprint outlining the techniques to help me and my team reflect on the factors that fuel our passion for patient care? Additionally, offer initial measures for short-term implementation. Segment your insights into distinct modules, each authenticated by corroborative evidence from credible sources. Explore unconventional approaches and diverse viewpoints. Let's examine each dimension meticulously. Write using an energizing tone and an engaging writing style.

Example 2: As a Leadership Coach in the technology industry, could you provide a thorough toolkit outlining the approaches I can employ to help my team reflect on the factors that fuel our passion for innovation? Additionally, offer immediate tactics for long-term implementation. Segment your insights into distinct modules, each endorsed with data from verified academic publications. Unearth hidden gems and non-traditional methods. Let's dissect this carefully. Write using an inspiring tone and an innovative writing style.

PROMPT No 83

Tags

Patience - Interactions - Self-Reflection

Goal

To delineate and establish structures that professionals can implement to foster patience in interactions with others, thereby enhancing interpersonal relationships and creating a conducive work environment.

Prompt

Act as a **Behavioral Consultant** specializing in **Emotional Intelligence** within the **legal industry**. Could you guide me through **a meticulous process to identify and establish the structures necessary for professionals to cultivate increased patience when interacting with others**? Please include **frameworks for self-reflection, strategies to manage reactions in challenging situations, and tools to monitor and enhance patience over time**. Ensure to cover how **to foster an organizational culture that values patience and understanding**. Explore **innovative or unconventional methodologies** to **accelerate the development of patience among professionals**. Your response should be comprehensive, leaving no important aspect unaddressed, and demonstrate an exceptional level of precision and quality. Let's think about this step by step. Write using a **constructive** tone and a **systematic, instructional** writing style.

Formula

Act as a **[profession]** specializing in **[area of expertise]** within the **[industry]**. Could you guide me through **[specific challenge/opportunity]**? Please include **[methods/techniques]**. Ensure to cover how **[key areas/topics]**. Explore **[exploratory direction]** to **[desired outcome]**. Your response should be comprehensive, leaving no important aspect unaddressed, and demonstrate an exceptional level of precision and quality. Let's think about this step by step. Write using a **[type]** tone and a **[style]** writing style.

Examples

Example 1: Act as a Communication Skills Trainer specializing in Conflict Resolution within the healthcare industry. Could you guide me through a structured approach for professionals to establish structures promoting patience in their interactions? Please include self-assessment tools, communication techniques for stressful scenarios, and feedback mechanisms to encourage patience. Make sure to cover how to create a supportive environment that values patience. Your response should be comprehensive, leaving no important aspect unaddressed, and demonstrate an exceptional level of precision and quality.

Let's think about this step by step. Write using a supportive tone and a clear, instructional writing style.

Example 2: Act as a Mindfulness Coach specializing in Stress Management within the education sector. Could you guide me through a comprehensive methodology for professionals to develop structures that foster patience with others? Please include mindfulness practices, emotional regulation strategies, and monitoring tools to track progress. Make sure to cover how to integrate these structures into daily professional interactions. Your response should be comprehensive, leaving no important aspect unaddressed, and demonstrate an exceptional level of precision and quality. Let's think about this step by step. Write using a calming tone and a methodical writing style.

PROMPT No 84

Tags

Empowerment - Self-efficacy - Motivation

Goal

To proficiently facilitate team members in recognizing and harnessing their intrinsic capabilities towards crafting the career trajectory they aspire to, thereby promoting self-efficacy, motivation, and career satisfaction.

Prompt

Act as a **Career Development Specialist** specializing in **Empowerment Strategies** within the **digital media industry**. Could you guide me through **an adept approach to assist my team in contemplating and accessing their own power to sculpt the career they desire**? Please include **frameworks for self-reflection, strategies for personal empowerment, and methodologies for aligning individual aspirations with actionable steps**. Ensure to cover how **to cultivate a supportive environment that encourages self-directed career development**. Probe into **innovative or unorthodox techniques** to **accentuate self-efficacy and proactive career management among team members**. Your response should be comprehensive, leaving no important aspect unaddressed, and demonstrate an exceptional level of precision and quality. Let's think about this step by step. Write using an **inspiring** tone and a **structured, instructional** writing style.

Formula

Act as a **[profession]** specializing in **[area of expertise]** within the **[industry]**. Could you guide me through **[specific challenge/opportunity]**? Please include **[methods/techniques]**. Ensure to cover how **[key areas/topics]**. Probe into **[exploratory direction]** to **[desired outcome]**. Your response should be comprehensive, leaving no important aspect unaddressed, and demonstrate an exceptional level of precision and quality. Let's think about this step by step. Write using a **[type]** tone and a **[style]** writing style.

Examples

Example 1: Act as a Personal Growth Facilitator specializing in Self-Efficacy Enhancement within the manufacturing industry. Could you guide me through an effective process to aid my team in recognizing and leveraging their inherent capabilities to build the career path they envision? Please include self-discovery exercises, empowerment techniques, and strategies for setting and pursuing career objectives. Make sure to cover how to instill a culture of continuous personal and professional growth. Your response should be comprehensive, leaving no important aspect unaddressed, and demonstrate an exceptional level of precision and quality. Let's think about this step by step. Write using an empowering tone and a clear, instructional writing style.

Example 2: Act as an Employee Engagement Consultant specializing in Career Self-Management within the e-commerce industry. Could you guide me through a nuanced approach to assisting my team in tapping into their own power to craft the career they long for? Please include introspective frameworks, strategies for self-empowerment, and methods for aligning personal ambitions with organizational opportunities. Make sure to cover how to foster an environment that nurtures autonomy and self-driven career progression. Your response should be comprehensive, leaving no important aspect unaddressed, and demonstrate an exceptional level of precision and quality. Let's think about this step by step. Write using a motivational tone and a step-by-step instructional writing style.

PROMPT No 85

<table>
<tr><td colspan="2" align="center">Tags</td></tr>
<tr><td colspan="2" align="center">Resources - Implementation - Performance</td></tr>
<tr><td colspan="2" align="center">Goal</td></tr>
<tr><td colspan="2">To identify and evaluate the essential resources that could enhance the performance and satisfaction of your team. These resources may range from software tools to training programs, and from flexible work arrangements to mental health support systems.</td></tr>
<tr><td colspan="2" align="center">Prompt</td></tr>
<tr><td colspan="2">Act as a **leadership coach** with a specialization in **resource optimization** for the **healthcare industry**. Could you guide me through **the identification and implementation of valuable resources that can assist my team in delivering top-tier performance**? Please include a **discussion on technological, educational, and emotional resources**. Make sure to cover how **the selected resources will fit within the work ecosystem and any potential constraints**. Explore unconventional solutions and alternative perspectives to continually refine our approach to resource allocation. Let's dissect this in a structured manner. Write using a **strategic** tone and a **problem-solving** writing style.</td></tr>
<tr><td colspan="2" align="center">Formula</td></tr>
<tr><td colspan="2">Act as a [profession] with a specialization in [area of expertise] for the [industry]. Could you guide me through [specific challenge/opportunity]? Please include [methods/techniques]. Make sure to cover how [key areas/topics]. Explore unconventional solutions and alternative perspectives to continually refine our approach to resource allocation. Let's dissect this in a structured manner. Write using a [type] tone and [style] writing style.</td></tr>
<tr><td colspan="2" align="center">Examples</td></tr>
<tr><td colspan="2">**Example 1**: Act as a productivity consultant with a specialization in digital tool utilization for the advertising industry. Could you assist me in sourcing and evaluating digital resources that can augment my team's productivity and creativity? Include a breakdown of budget-friendly and premium options. Make sure to discuss the ease of integration into our existing tech stack. Delve into uncharted territories and groundbreaking concepts to keep us ahead of the curve. Write using an innovative tone and a how-to writing style.
Example 2: Act as an HR specialist with a specialization in employee well-being for the education sector. Can you help me identify resources aimed at enhancing my team's emotional and mental health? Please include actionable steps to introduce these resources and gauge their effectiveness over time. Make sure to elaborate on how such resources can contribute to the overall work environment. Conduct an intensive and all-inclusive study to ensure long-term benefits. Write using an empathetic tone and a comprehensive writing style.</td></tr>
</table>

PROMPT No 86

Futurist - Brainstorming - Innovation

Goal

To obtain a comprehensive, actionable guide on methods for facilitating a thought experiment within a team to explore what could be achieved if they had unlimited time and resources, with the aim of unlocking latent potential and inspiring innovative thinking.

Prompt

As a **Futurist Consultant** in the **technology sector**, could you provide an exhaustive guide outlining the methods **my team** and I can employ to imagine what we could achieve in **our** work if we had **unlimited time and resources**? Please include both **brainstorming techniques** and **analytical frameworks**. Segment the guide into **distinct categories**, and substantiate each with **empirical data and scholarly references**. Explore unconventional approaches and diverse viewpoints. Let's dissect this carefully. Write using an **analytical** tone and a **structured** writing style.

Formula

As a **[profession]** in the **[industry]**, could you provide an exhaustive guide outlining the methods **[I/Name/Role]** and **[my/our/their]** **[team/group/department]** can employ to imagine what we could achieve in **[our/their]** work if we had **[unlimited time and resources/other hypothetical scenarios]**? Please include both **[brainstorming techniques/analytical frameworks]**. Segment the guide into **[distinct categories]**, and substantiate each with **[empirical data/scholarly references]**. Explore unconventional approaches and diverse viewpoints. Let's dissect this carefully. Write using a **[type]** tone and **[style]** writing style.

Examples

Example 1: As an Innovation Coach in the healthcare industry, could you provide an exhaustive guide outlining the methods a research team and their manager can employ to imagine what they could achieve in medical research if they had unlimited time and resources? Please include both mind-mapping exercises and SWOT analyses. Divide the guide into key areas, and validate each with clinical studies and peer-reviewed articles. Investigate unexpected avenues and creative pathways. Let's examine each dimension meticulously. Write using a focused tone and a concise writing style.

Example 2: As a Leadership Development Consultant in the manufacturing sector, could you provide an exhaustive guide outlining the methods my production team and I can employ to imagine what we could achieve in product development if we had unlimited time and resources? Please include both ideation sessions and feasibility studies. Break the guide into actionable steps, and corroborate each with industry benchmarks and case studies. Unearth hidden gems and non-traditional methods. Let's tackle this in a phased manner. Write using a balanced tone and a nuanced writing style.

SELF-ASSESSMENT

PROMPT No 87

Introspection - Decision-making - Behavior

Goal

To provide leaders with a nuanced and actionable framework that enables their teams to engage in deep self-reflection, focusing on understanding their core identity and essence, which in turn informs their professional behavior and decision-making.

Act as a **Personal Development Coach** specializing in the **technology sector**. Could you outline a **structured approach** for **guiding** my team in **reflecting** on their **core identity** and **understanding who they are at their essence**? Include **exercises, questionnaires, and other tools** that **facilitate** this **introspective** process. Let's methodically dissect each component. Your response should be comprehensive, leaving no important aspect unaddressed, and demonstrate an exceptional level of precision and quality. Write using an **introspective** tone and an **analytical** writing style.

Act as a **[profession]** specializing in the **[industry]**. Could you outline a **[structured/comprehensive]** approach for **[guiding/leading]** my team in **[reflecting on/understanding]** their **[core identity/true essence]?** Include **[exercises/questionnaires/tools]** that **[facilitate/enable]** this **[introspective/deep]** process. Let's methodically dissect each component. Your response should be comprehensive, leaving no important aspect unaddressed, and demonstrate an exceptional level of precision and quality. Write using a **[type]** tone and **[style]** writing style.

Example 1: Act as a Leadership Consultant specializing in the finance industry. Could you provide a comprehensive guide for assisting my team in introspection about their core identity? Include reflective exercises and self-assessment tools that can be used to facilitate this process. Let's sequentially address each element. Your response should be comprehensive, leaving no important aspect unaddressed, and demonstrate an exceptional level of precision and quality. Write using a contemplative tone and a reflective writing style.

Example 2: Act as a Team Development Specialist specializing in the healthcare sector. Could you delineate a structured methodology for helping my team understand who they are at their essence? Include guided meditation sessions and psychological questionnaires as tools for this exploration. Let's tackle this in a phased manner. Your response should be comprehensive, leaving no important aspect unaddressed, and demonstrate an exceptional level of precision and quality. Write using an empathetic tone and a human-centered writing style.

PROMPT No 88

Evolution - Mentoring - Perspectives

To equip leaders with a robust methodology for tracking and understanding the evolution of their team's perspectives on responsibilities and potential, thereby enabling more effective coaching, mentoring, and talent development strategies.

Act as an **Organizational Development Specialist** specializing in the **retail industry**. Could you provide a **comprehensive** framework for **examining** how my team's perspective on their **responsibilities evolves** over **time**? Include **qualitative assessment methods**, as well as **strategies** for capturing temporal changes for **assessment**. Let's methodically dissect each component. Your response should be comprehensive, leaving no important aspect unaddressed, and demonstrate an exceptional level of precision and quality. Write using an **analytical** tone and a **structured** writing style.

Act as a **[profession]** specializing in the **[industry]**. Could you provide a **[comprehensive/robust/detailed]** framework for **[examining/assessing/evaluating]** how my team's perspective on their **[responsibilities/potential/roles]** **[evolves/changes/shifts]** over **[time/periods/phases]**? Include **[qualitative/quantitative assessment methods/strategies]** for capturing **[temporal changes/psychological metrics]** for **[assessment/evaluation]**. Let's methodically dissect each component. Your response should be comprehensive, leaving no important aspect unaddressed, and demonstrate an exceptional level of precision and quality. Write using a **[type]** tone and **[style]** writing style.

Example 1: Act as a Talent Development Coach specializing in the tech industry. Could you offer a robust framework for assessing how software engineers' perspectives on their roles and potential change over the course of a project? Include performance metrics, self-assessment tools, and peer reviews. Let's sequentially address each element. Your response should be comprehensive, leaving no important aspect unaddressed, and demonstrate an exceptional level of precision and quality. Write using a data-driven tone and an informative writing style.

Example 2: Act as a Leadership Consultant specializing in the non-profit sector. Could you delineate a detailed methodology for evaluating how my team's view on their responsibilities evolves during a fundraising campaign? Include donor engagement metrics, team surveys, and one-on-one interviews. Let's tackle this in a phased manner. Your response should be comprehensive, leaving no important aspect unaddressed, and demonstrate an exceptional level of precision and quality. Write using an empathetic tone and a consultative writing style.

PROMPT No 89

Feedback - Communication - Motivations

To adeptly discern the core values, aspirations, and motivations that significantly matter to the team in their work or within the company, fostering a conducive environment for engagement, satisfaction, and meaningful contributions.

Act as an **Organizational Values Analyst** specializing in **Employee Engagement** within the **automotive sector**. Could you guide me through **an intricate approach to identifying what truly matters to my team in their work or within the company**? Please include **methods for value discovery, effective communication channels, and feedback gathering techniques**. Make sure to cover how **to create a safe and open environment that encourages honest expression**. Explore **novel and empathetic ways** to **delve into the team's core motivations and aspirations**. Your response should be comprehensive, leaving no important aspect unaddressed, and demonstrate an exceptional level of precision and quality. Let's think about this step by step. Write using an **insightful** tone and a **guided, explorative** writing style.

Act as a **[profession]** specializing in **[area of expertise]** within the **[industry]**. Could you guide me through **[specific challenge/opportunity]**? Please include **[methods/techniques]**.

Make sure to cover how **[key areas/topics]**. Explore **[exploratory direction]** to **[desired outcome]**. Your response should be comprehensive, leaving no important aspect unaddressed, and demonstrate an exceptional level of precision and quality. Let's think about this step by step. Write using a **[type]** tone and a **[style]** writing style.

Example 1: Act as a Team Dynamics Specialist specializing in Motivational Analysis within the aerospace sector. Could you guide me through a thorough process to identify what genuinely matters to my team in their professional endeavors or within our company? Please include motivational assessment tools, interactive workshops, and reflective exercises. Make sure to cover how to foster a culture of open dialogue and mutual respect. Your response should be comprehensive, leaving no important aspect unaddressed, and demonstrate an exceptional level of precision and quality. Let's think about this step by step. Write using an engaging tone and a reflective, instructive writing style.

Example 2: Act as an Employee Engagement Expert specializing in Value Alignment within the pharmaceutical sector. Could you guide me through an in-depth approach to discerning the core values and driving factors that significantly matter to my team in their work or within our organization? Please include values identification surveys, focus group discussions, and one-on-one interviews. Make sure to cover how to ensure anonymity and trust during the feedback gathering process. Your response should be comprehensive, leaving no important aspect unaddressed, and demonstrate an exceptional level of precision and quality. Let's think about this step by step. Write using a respectful tone and a methodical, elucidative writing style.

SKILLS

PROMPT No 90

Acquisition - Performance - Alignment

To meticulously devise an efficient, well-structured approach for acquiring new skills necessary for your team, ensuring this acquisition enhances overall team performance, and aligns with strategic objectives.

As a **Skill Development Strategist** specializing in **Effective Learning Pathways** within the **Management Consulting industry**, how can I meticulously devise and execute a well-structured, efficient approach for identifying and acquiring new skills crucial for my team, ensuring that this acquisition significantly amplifies overall team performance and aligns seamlessly with our strategic objectives? I am seeking an in-depth discussion outlining robust methodologies, actionable strategies, and measurable metrics, as well as the potential implications of such skill acquisition on **team dynamics, organizational alignment, and competitive advantage**. The discourse should encapsulate every critical facet of this endeavor with an exceptional degree of precision and quality.

As a **[Profession]** specializing in **[Specialization]** within the **[Industry]**, how can I meticulously devise and execute a well-structured, efficient approach for identifying and acquiring new skills crucial for my team, ensuring that this acquisition significantly amplifies overall team performance and aligns seamlessly with our strategic objectives? I am seeking an in-depth discussion outlining robust methodologies, actionable strategies, and measurable metrics, as well as the potential implications of such skill acquisition on **[team dynamics/organizational alignment/competitive advantage or other relevant impact areas]**. The discourse should encapsulate every critical facet of this endeavor with an exceptional degree of precision and quality.

Example 1: As a Talent Enhancement Architect specializing in Skill Augmentation Pathways within the Financial Services industry, how can I meticulously devise and execute a well-structured, efficient approach for identifying and acquiring new skills crucial for my team, ensuring that this acquisition significantly amplifies overall team performance and aligns seamlessly with our strategic objectives? I am seeking an in-depth discussion outlining robust methodologies, actionable strategies, and measurable metrics, as well as the potential implications of such skill acquisition on team cohesion, client satisfaction, and market positioning. The discourse should encapsulate every critical facet of this endeavor with an exceptional degree of precision and quality.

Example 2: As a Capability Expansion Advisor specializing in Performance-Driven Learning within the Health Tech industry, how can I meticulously devise and execute a well-structured, efficient approach for identifying and acquiring new skills crucial for my team, ensuring that this acquisition significantly amplifies overall team performance and aligns seamlessly with our strategic objectives? I am seeking an in-depth discussion outlining robust methodologies, actionable strategies, and measurable metrics, as well as the potential implications of such skill acquisition on product innovation, regulatory compliance, and patient satisfaction. The discourse should encapsulate every critical facet of this endeavor with an exceptional degree of precision and quality.

STRATEGIES

PROMPT No 91

Recognition - Resilience - Acknowledgment

To acquire a comprehensive, actionable guide on methods for genuinely acknowledging a team's courage or commitment, even when their strategy doesn't yield the desired outcome, with the aim of fostering resilience, team cohesion, and a culture of continuous improvement.

As an Organizational Psychologist in the e-commerce industry, could you provide an exhaustive guide outlining the methods I can employ to genuinely acknowledge my team for their courage or commitment, even if their strategy doesn't yield the desired outcome? Please include both verbal and non-verbal recognition techniques. Segment the guide into distinct categories, and substantiate each with empirical data and scholarly references. Explore unconventional approaches and diverse viewpoints. Let's dissect this carefully. Write using an analytical tone and a structured writing style.

As a **[profession]** in the **[industry]**, could you provide an exhaustive guide outlining the methods **[I/Name/Role]** can employ to genuinely acknowledge **[my/our/their]** **[team/group/department]** for their **[courage or commitment/specific quality]**, even if their strategy doesn't yield the **[desired outcome/specific goal]**? Please include both

[verbal/non-verbal recognition techniques]. Segment the guide into **[distinct categories]**, and substantiate each with **[empirical data/scholarly references]**. Explore unconventional approaches and diverse viewpoints. Let's dissect this carefully. Write using a **[type]** tone and **[style]** writing style.

Example 1: As a Leadership Coach in the healthcare industry, could you provide an exhaustive guide outlining the methods a department head can employ to genuinely acknowledge their medical staff for their courage or commitment, even if a new patient care strategy doesn't yield the desired patient satisfaction scores? Please include both public commendations and private feedback sessions. Divide the guide into key areas, and validate each with clinical studies and peer-reviewed articles. Investigate unexpected avenues and creative pathways. Let's examine each dimension meticulously. Write using a focused tone and a concise writing style.

Example 2: As a Team Development Specialist in the manufacturing sector, could you provide an exhaustive guide outlining the methods I can employ to genuinely acknowledge my assembly line workers for their commitment, even if a new production technique doesn't yield the expected efficiency gains? Please include both team meetings and individual recognition awards. Break the guide into actionable steps, and corroborate each with industry benchmarks and case studies. Unearth hidden gems and non-traditional methods. Let's tackle this in a phased manner. Write using a balanced tone and a nuanced writing style.

PROMPT No 92

Effectiveness - ROI - Decision-making

To provide business leaders with a rigorous methodology for evaluating the effectiveness and efficiency of various strategies or plans, aimed at ensuring alignment with company objectives and maximizing ROI.

Act as a **Strategic Planning Advisor** specializing in the **automotive industry**. Could you **elucidate** the most **optimal methods** for **assessing** which **strategy** will be most **effective and efficient** in **achieving** my company's **objectives**? Include **decision-making frameworks, key performance indicators, and risk assessment tools**. Let's systematically explore each facet. Your response should be comprehensive, leaving no important aspect unaddressed, and demonstrate an exceptional level of precision and quality. Write using a **data-driven** tone and a **structured** writing style.

Act as a **[profession]** specializing in the **[industry]**. Could you **[elucidate/explain/outline]** the most **[optimal/effective/efficient]** **[methods/techniques/approaches]** for **[assessing/evaluating/measuring]** which **[strategy/plan/approach]** will be most **[effective/efficient/successful]** in **[achieving/meeting/fulfilling]** my company's **[objectives/goals/targets]**? Include **[decision-making frameworks/key performance indicators/risk assessment tools]** for **[evaluation/assessment/analysis]**. Let's systematically explore each facet. Your response should be comprehensive, leaving no important aspect unaddressed, and demonstrate an exceptional level of precision and quality. Write using a **[type]** tone and **[style]** writing style.

Example 1: Act as a Business Strategy Consultant specializing in the healthcare industry. Could you outline the most effective methods for assessing which operational plan will be most efficient in achieving my hospital's patient care objectives? Include cost-benefit analyses, patient satisfaction metrics, and compliance checks. Let's sequentially address each element. Your response should be comprehensive, leaving no important aspect unaddressed, and demonstrate an exceptional level of precision and quality. Write using an analytical tone and a detailed writing style.

Example 2: Act as a Corporate Strategy Analyst specializing in the software industry. Could you explain the most efficient techniques for evaluating which product development strategy will be most effective in achieving my company's market share objectives? Include A/B testing, customer feedback loops, and scalability assessments. Let's tackle this in a phased manner. Your response should be comprehensive, leaving no important aspect unaddressed, and demonstrate an exceptional level of precision and quality. Write using a data-driven tone and a structured writing style.

STRENGTH

PROMPT No 93

Tags

Attraction - Roles - Inherent

Goal

To equip leaders with a robust analytical framework that allows them to interpret their team's consistent attraction to specific roles or tasks as indicators of inherent strengths, thereby facilitating more effective team management and individual development.

Prompt

Act as an **Organizational Behavior Analyst** specializing in the **construction industry**. Could you **elucidate** the **analytical methods** for **interpreting my** team's consistent attraction to **certain roles or tasks** as indicators of their **inherent** strengths? Include **both qualitative and quantitative assessment techniques**. Let's methodically dissect each component. Your response should be comprehensive, leaving no important aspect unaddressed, and demonstrate an exceptional level of precision and quality. Write using a **diagnostic** tone and an **evidence-based** writing style.

Formula

Act as a **[profession]** specializing in the **[industry]**. Could you **[elucidate/explain/provide]** **[analytical/interpretive/assessment]** **[methods/mechanisms/frameworks]** for **[interpreting/understanding/analyzing]** **[my/our/the]** team's consistent attraction to **[certain/specific/individual]** **[roles/tasks/positions]** as indicators of their **[inherent/natural/latent]** strengths? Include **[both/and/or]** **[qualitative/quantitative/mixed]** **[assessment/evaluation/measurement]** **[techniques/methods/tools]**. Let's **[methodically dissect each component/systematically explore each facet]**. Let's methodically dissect each component. Your response should be comprehensive, leaving no important aspect unaddressed, and demonstrate an exceptional level of precision and quality. Write using a **[type]** tone and **[style]** writing style.

Examples

Example 1: Act as a Team Dynamics Specialist specializing in the software development industry. Could you provide a structured methodology for understanding my development team's consistent attraction to specific coding tasks as indicators of their natural strengths? Include data-driven metrics and peer-review methods. Let's examine each dimension meticulously. Your response should be comprehensive, leaving no important aspect unaddressed, and demonstrate an exceptional level of precision and quality. Write using an analytical tone and a data-centric writing style.

Example 2: Act as a Leadership Coach specializing in the healthcare sector. Could you elucidate the assessment techniques for interpreting my medical staff's consistent attraction to certain patient-care roles as indicators of their inherent strengths? Include observational studies and self-assessment tools. Let's deconstruct this subject stepwise. Your response should be comprehensive, leaving no important aspect unaddressed, and demonstrate an exceptional level of precision and quality. Write using an empathetic tone and a patient-focused writing style.

PROMPT No 94

Tags
Strengths - Productivity - Morale

Goal
To identify robust methodologies that facilitate the comprehensive listing and nuanced description of team strengths for enhanced productivity and morale.

Prompt
As a **Professional Team Coach** specializing in **team dynamics** within the **healthcare industry**, provide an exhaustive and meticulous examination, incorporating innovative insights and inventive strategies for **utilizing** methodologies that allow my team to **list** and **describe** their strengths **comprehensively**. Discuss the implications of these methods on **team productivity and morale**.

Formula
As a **[profession]** specializing in **[area of expertise/focus]** within the **[industry]**, provide an exhaustive and meticulous examination, incorporating innovative insights and inventive strategies for **[utilizing/applying/implementing]** methodologies that allow my team to **[list/enumerate/catalog]** and **[describe/explain/characterize]** their strengths **[comprehensively/fully/thoroughly]**. Discuss the **[implications/consequences/effects]** of these methods on **[team productivity/morale/team dynamics]**.

Examples

Example 1: As a Scrum Master specializing in agile methodologies within the technology sector, provide an exhaustive and meticulous examination, incorporating innovative insights and inventive strategies for applying methodologies that allow your team to enumerate and explain their strengths fully. Discuss the consequences of these methods on team productivity.

Example 2: As a Team Leader specializing in leadership development within the non-profit sector, provide an exhaustive and meticulous examination, incorporating innovative insights and inventive strategies for implementing methodologies that allow your team to catalog and characterize their strengths thoroughly. Discuss the effects of these methods on team morale.

PROMPT No 95

Development - Strengths - Metrics

To create a comprehensive development plan that identifies, leverages, and continuously refines the individual and collective strengths of your team, thereby driving performance, engagement, and overall business results.

As a **project manager** specializing in **data analytics** within the **automotive industry,** provide an exhaustive and meticulous examination, incorporating innovative insights and inventive strategies for **establishing a comprehensive development plan that identifies and leverages your team's key strengths in data interpretation, client interaction, and problem-solving**. Further, explore how to integrate this strengths-based approach into your **team's quarterly objectives and performance metrics**.

As a **[profession]** specializing in **[area of expertise/focus]** within the **[industry]**, provide an exhaustive and meticulous examination, incorporating innovative insights and inventive strategies for **[establishing a comprehensive development plan that identifies and leverages your team's key strengths in various competencies]**. Further, explore how to integrate this strengths-based approach into your **[quarterly objectives/performance metrics/ongoing projects]**.

Example 1: As an engineering manager specializing in renewable energy within the utilities sector, provide an exhaustive and meticulous examination, incorporating innovative insights and inventive strategies, to formulate a development plan that leverages your team's strengths in project management and innovative design. Further, explore how to incorporate this strengths-based approach into your team's sustainability initiatives and yearly goals.

Example 2: As a marketing director specializing in digital campaigns within the retail industry, provide an exhaustive and meticulous examination, incorporating innovative insights and inventive strategies, to create a development plan that accentuates your team's strengths in customer engagement and data-driven decision-making. Further, explore how to weave this strengths-based approach into your upcoming product launches and consumer research.

PROMPT No 96

Strengths - Performance - Methodology

To provide leaders with a robust methodology for leveraging their team's inherent strengths in a targeted manner to accelerate progress towards organizational goals or objectives, thereby enhancing team performance and job satisfaction.

Act as an **Organizational Development Consultant** specializing in the **fintech industry**. Could you **delineate** a **comprehensive approach** for **exploring** ways to **utilize** my team's **strengths** to **propel** them towards **achieving** their **goals or objectives**? Include **evidence-based strategies, key performance indicators, and potential pitfalls to avoid.**

Let's **think about this step by step**. Write using a **growth-oriented** tone and **expansion-minded** writing style.

Act as a **[profession]** specializing in the **[industry]**. Could you **[delineate/outline/detail]** a **[comprehensive/robust/structured]** **[approach/methodology/plan]** for **[exploring/investigating/identifying]** ways to **[utilize/leverage/employ]** my team's **[strengths/capabilities/talents]** to **[propel/accelerate/drive]** them towards **[achieving/meeting/reaching]** their **[goals/objectives/targets]**? Include **[evidence-based strategies/research-backed methods]**, **[key performance indicators/metrics/benchmarks]**, and **[potential pitfalls/challenges]** to **[avoid/mitigate]**. Let's **[think about this step by step/methodically dissect each component]**. Write using a **[type]** tone and **[style]** writing style.

Example 1: Act as a Talent Management Specialist specializing in the retail industry. Could you outline a robust plan for identifying ways to leverage my team's capabilities to accelerate them towards meeting their quarterly sales targets? Include research-backed methods, key metrics, and challenges to mitigate. Let's scrutinize this topic incrementally. Write using a results-driven tone and performance-focused writing style.

Example 2: Act as a Leadership Coach specializing in the manufacturing sector. Could you detail a structured methodology for investigating how to employ my team's talents to drive them towards achieving their efficiency objectives? Include evidence-based strategies, key performance indicators, and potential pitfalls to avoid. Let's carefully evaluate each segment. Write using a strategic tone and forward-thinking writing style.

PROMPT No 97

Consequences - Strengths - Mitigation

To equip leaders with a nuanced framework for reflecting on and mitigating any unintended consequences that may arise from leveraging their team's strengths, thereby ensuring a balanced and sustainable approach to team development and performance optimization.

Act as a Risk Management Consultant specializing in the software development industry. Could you provide a detailed reflection on any unintended consequences that may arise from the use of my team's strengths? Include risk assessment methodologies, potential impact on team dynamics, and actionable mitigation strategies. Let's think about this step by step. Write using a cautionary tone and risk-averse writing style.

Act as a **[profession]** specializing in the **[industry]**. Could you provide a **[detailed/comprehensive/thorough]** **[reflection/analysis/evaluation]** on any **[unintended consequences/unforeseen risks/unexpected outcomes]** that may **[arise/emerge/occur]** from the **[use/application/employment]** of my team's **[strengths/skills/talents]**? Include **[risk assessment methodologies/evaluation techniques]**, **[potential impact/effects]** on **[team dynamics/organizational culture]**, and **[actionable mitigation strategies/contingency plans]**. Let's **[think about this step by step/methodically dissect each component]**. Write using a **[type]** tone and **[style]** writing style.

Example 1: Act as a Human Resources Analyst specializing in the healthcare sector. Could you provide a comprehensive analysis on any unforeseen risks that may emerge from the application of my team's skills? Include risk assessment techniques, potential effects on team morale, and actionable mitigation strategies. Let's carefully evaluate each segment. Write using a quality-focused tone and meticulous writing style.

Example 2: Act as an Organizational Behaviorist specializing in the logistics industry. Could you provide a thorough reflection on any unexpected outcomes that may occur from the use of my team's talents? Include evaluation techniques, potential impact on organizational culture, and contingency plans. Let's systematically explore each facet. Write using a transparent tone and open writing style.

PROMPT No 98

Tags

Optimization - Strengths - Stakeholders

Goal

To systematically identify and deploy high-impact strategies that optimize the unique strengths of each team member, thereby amplifying overall team performance, engagement, and effectiveness in achieving organizational goals.

Prompt

As a **team leader** specializing in **organizational development** within the **healthcare industry**, provide an exhaustive and meticulous examination, incorporating innovative insights and inventive strategies, for discovering methodologies to leverage individual and collective strengths of your team in **patient care, resource management, and organizational leadership**. Also, delve into how to communicate these plans through different team layers to secure buy-in from stakeholders.

Formula

As a **[profession]** specializing in **[area of expertise/focus]** within the **[industry]**, provide an exhaustive and meticulous examination, incorporating innovative insights and inventive strategies, for discovering methodologies to leverage individual and collective strengths of your team in **[specific operational areas]**. Also, delve into how to communicate these plans through different team layers to secure buy-in from stakeholders.

Examples

Example 1: As a Sales Director specializing in consumer electronics within the retail sector, provide an exhaustive and meticulous examination, incorporating innovative insights and inventive strategies, for uncovering best practices to capitalize on the unique talents and skills of your sales team in areas like customer engagement, upselling, and retention. Also, delve into how to communicate these plans through different team layers to secure buy-in from stakeholders.

Example 2: As a CTO specializing in cybersecurity within the IT industry, provide an exhaustive and meticulous examination, incorporating innovative insights and inventive strategies, for devising a comprehensive approach to leverage the technical and soft skills of your engineering team in the domains of network security, system architecture, and client interactions. Also, delve into how to communicate these plans through different team layers to secure buy-in from stakeholders.

PROMPT No 99

Opportunities - Skill-Gap - Metrics

Goal

To provide team leaders, managers, and organizational decision-makers with a comprehensive methodology for identifying opportunities where team members can practice and apply specific strengths, thereby enhancing skill mastery, job satisfaction, and overall team performance.

Prompt

Act as a **Talent Optimization Consultant** with a specialization in **strength-based development** in the **manufacturing industry**. Could you guide me through **a detailed strategy to identify opportunities where my team can practice and apply a specific strength**? Please include **opportunity mapping, skill-gap analysis, and project alignment techniques**. Make sure to cover how **to evaluate the impact of these opportunities on team dynamics and organizational goals**. Investigate unconventional **training methods** and cutting-edge **performance metrics** to **measure skill application effectively**. Your response should be comprehensive, leaving no important aspect unaddressed, and demonstrate an exceptional level of precision and quality. Let's think about this step by step. Write using a **strategic** tone and an **actionable** plan style.

Formula

Act as a **[profession]** with a specialization in **[area of expertise]** in the **[industry]**. Could you guide me through **[specific challenge/opportunity]**? Please include **[methods/techniques]**. **Make sure to cover how [key areas/topics]**. Investigate unconventional **[area for innovation]** and cutting-edge **[technologies/methods]** to **[desired outcome]**. Your response should be comprehensive, leaving no important aspect unaddressed, and demonstrate an exceptional level of precision and quality. Let's think about this step by step. Write using a **[type]** tone and **[style]** writing style.

Examples

Example 1: Act as a Leadership Coach with a specialization in team dynamics in the healthcare industry. Could you guide me through a comprehensive approach to identify opportunities where my nursing staff can practice and apply their patient care strengths? Please include patient case studies, peer reviews, and simulation exercises. Make sure to cover how to integrate these opportunities into daily workflows and how to measure their impact on patient outcomes. Explore the use of virtual reality training and real-time feedback systems to enhance skill application. Your response should be comprehensive, leaving no important aspect unaddressed, and demonstrate an exceptional level of precision and quality. Let's think about this step by step. Write using a supportive tone and a coaching guide style.
Example 2: Act as a Business Analyst with a specialization in project management in the tech industry. Could you guide me through a data-driven plan to identify opportunities where my software development team can practice and apply their coding strengths? Please include sprint planning, code reviews, and hackathons. Make sure to cover how to align these opportunities with project milestones and how to quantify their impact on project timelines. Delve into agile methodologies and DevOps practices to optimize skill application. Your response should be comprehensive, leaving no important aspect unaddressed, and demonstrate an exceptional level of precision and quality. Let's think about this step by step. Write using an analytical tone and a project blueprint style.

PROMPT No 100

Tags

Sales Targets - KPIs - Risk Mitigation

Goal

To equip leaders with a comprehensive toolkit for identifying actionable steps that will propel their teams toward achieving specific results or sales targets, thereby enhancing organizational performance and revenue.

Prompt

Act as a **Sales Strategy Consultant** specializing in the **SaaS industry**. Could you **elucidate a detailed plan** for **identifying** the **actions** that will move my team closer to **achieving our sales targets**? Include **key performance indicators, actionable tactics,** and **risk mitigation strategies**. Let's **think about this step by step**. Write using a **results-driven** tone and **performance-focused** writing style.

Formula

Act as a **[profession]** specializing in the **[industry]**. Could you **[elucidate/outline/detail]** a **[detailed/comprehensive/structured]** **[plan/strategy/framework]** for **[identifying/ascertaining/determining]** the **[actions/steps/measures]** that will move my team closer to **[achieving/reaching/meeting]** our **[sales targets/results/objectives]**? Include **[key performance indicators/metrics/benchmarks], [actionable tactics/feasible strategies/practical steps],** and **[risk mitigation strategies/contingency plans]**. Let's **[think about this step by step/systematically explore each facet]**. Write using a **[type]** tone and **[style]** writing style.

Examples

Example 1: Act as a Business Development Specialist specializing in the healthcare industry. Could you outline a comprehensive strategy for identifying the steps that will move my team closer to meeting our quarterly revenue goals? Include key metrics, practical steps, and contingency plans for unforeseen challenges. Let's examine each dimension meticulously. Write using a strategic tone and a forward-thinking writing style.

Example 2: Act as a Performance Coach specializing in the automotive sector. Could you detail a structured framework for ascertaining the actions that will propel my team toward achieving our customer retention targets? Include benchmarks, actionable tactics, and risk mitigation strategies for market fluctuations. Let's carefully evaluate each segment. Write using an analytical tone and a systematic writing style.

PROMPT No 101

Tags

Work Arrangements - Team Survey - KPI Alignment

Goal

To provide a robust methodology for exploring alternative options or arrangements in work schedules or environments that would better serve their teams, thereby enhancing productivity, well-being, and overall team cohesion.

Prompt

Act as a **Workplace Design Consultant** with a specialization in **flexible work arrangements in the renewable energy industry**. Could you guide me through **a comprehensive strategy to explore alternative options or arrangements for the current work schedule or work environment that would better serve my team**? Please include **time management frameworks, ergonomic considerations, and remote work policies**. Make sure to cover how **to conduct a team survey for preferences and how to align these alternatives with organizational KPIs**. Investigate unconventional **work arrangements** and cutting-edge **workspace technologies** to **maximize team satisfaction and productivity**. Your response should be comprehensive, leaving no important aspect unaddressed, and demonstrate an exceptional level of precision and quality. Let's think about this step by step. Write using an **innovative** tone and a **change management** style.

Act as a **[profession]** with a specialization in **[area of expertise]** in the **[industry]**. Could you guide me through **[specific challenge/opportunity]**? Please include **[methods/techniques]**. Make sure to cover how **[key areas/topics]**. Investigate unconventional **[area for innovation]** and cutting-edge **[technologies/methods]** to **[desired outcome]**. Your response should be comprehensive, leaving no important aspect unaddressed, and demonstrate an exceptional level of precision and quality. Let's think about this step by step. Write using a **[type]** tone and **[style]** writing style.

Example 1: Act as an HR Innovator with a specialization in work-life balance in the tech industry. Could you guide me through a structured plan to explore alternative work schedules that would better serve my software development team? Please include flextime options, compressed workweeks, and asynchronous communication protocols. Make sure to cover how to assess team members' time zone differences and how to measure the impact on project timelines. Explore the use of AI-driven scheduling tools and virtual reality meeting spaces to enhance team collaboration. Your response should be comprehensive, leaving no important aspect unaddressed, and demonstrate an exceptional level of precision and quality. Let's think about this step by step. Write using a forward-thinking tone and a digital transformation style.

Example 2: Act as an Environmental Psychologist with a specialization in workspace design in the healthcare industry. Could you guide me through a methodical approach to explore alternative work environments that would better serve my nursing staff? Please include lighting considerations, noise control, and break room amenities. Make sure to cover how to evaluate the current stress levels of the team and how to align new environments with patient care objectives. Delve into biophilic design elements and smart building technologies to improve staff well-being. Your response should be comprehensive, leaving no important aspect unaddressed, and demonstrate an exceptional level of precision and quality. Let's think about this step by step. Write using a holistic tone and a well-being optimization style.

PROMPT No 102

Strategy - Stakeholders - Collaboration

To furnish leaders, project managers, and individual contributors with an exhaustive methodology for developing a strategic plan aimed at garnering essential support for key priorities. This will encompass communication tactics, collaboration frameworks, and alternative avenues to ensure the successful execution of these priorities.

Act as a **Strategic Planning Consultant** with expertise in **stakeholder management** in the **energy sector**. Could you guide me through **a comprehensive plan to secure the necessary support for my key priorities**? Please include **communication blueprints, collaboration models, and risk mitigation strategies**. Make sure to cover how **to identify and engage critical stakeholders, both internal and external**. Investigate unconventional methods and creative solutions to **ensure robust support and successful outcomes**. Your response should be comprehensive, leaving no important aspect unaddressed, and demonstrate an exceptional level of precision and quality. Let's think about this step by step. Write using a **tactical** tone and a **project plan** writing style.

Act as a **[profession]** with expertise in **[area of expertise]** in the **[industry]**. Could you guide me through **[specific challenge/opportunity]**? Please include **[methods/techniques]**. Make sure to cover how **[key areas/topics]**. Investigate unconventional methods and creative solutions to **[desired outcome]**. Your response should be comprehensive, leaving no important aspect unaddressed, and demonstrate an exceptional level of precision and quality. Let's think about this step by step. Write using a **[type]** tone and **[style]** writing style.

Example 1: Act as a Change Management Specialist with expertise in organizational alignment in the healthcare industry. Could you guide me through a detailed plan to obtain the necessary support for implementing a new electronic health record system? Please include communication strategies, cross-departmental collaboration frameworks, and contingency plans. Make sure to cover how to secure buy-in from medical staff, administrative personnel, and external vendors. Explore agile methodologies and change resistance mitigation to ensure smooth implementation. Your response should be comprehensive, leaving no important aspect unaddressed, and demonstrate an exceptional level of precision and quality. Let's think about this step by step. Write using a persuasive tone and a roadmap writing style.

Example 2: Act as a Business Analyst with expertise in resource allocation in the retail sector. Could you guide me through a plan to secure the necessary resources and support for launching a new product line? Please include stakeholder mapping, communication channels, and ROI projections. Make sure to cover how to engage with key decision-makers, suppliers, and marketing teams. Delve into data-driven approaches and gamification techniques to incentivize support. Your response should be comprehensive, leaving no important aspect unaddressed, and demonstrate an exceptional level of precision and quality. Let's think about this step by step. Write using an analytical tone and a business case writing style.

VALUES

PROMPT No 103

Values - Alignment - Communication

To incisively identify and effectively communicate the core values that resonate with your team members in their work environment, within the team dynamic, or in any specific project or context.

As a **team leader** specializing in **Organizational Development** within the **financial services industry**, provide an exhaustive and meticulous examination, incorporating innovative insights and inventive strategies for **determining and articulating the values your team holds dear in their daily tasks, team interactions, or specific project contexts**. Also, outline how these identified values align with **broader organizational goals**.

As a **[profession]** specializing in **[area of expertise/focus]** within the **[industry]**, provide an exhaustive and meticulous examination, incorporating innovative insights and inventive strategies for **[determining and articulating the values your team places on their work, interactions, or specific contexts]**. Also, outline how these identified values align with **[broader organizational goals/departmental objectives/corporate vision]**.

Example 1: As a product manager specializing in User Experience within the e-commerce sector, provide an exhaustive and meticulous examination, incorporating innovative insights and inventive strategies, to determine and articulate what your design team values in their creative process. Also, outline how these values align with the departmental objectives.

Example 2: As a nursing supervisor specializing in Palliative Care within a hospital, provide an exhaustive and meticulous examination, incorporating innovative insights and inventive strategies, to determine and articulate what your team values in patient care and team cooperation. Also, outline how these values align with the hospital's vision for patient-centered care.

PROMPT No 104

Embrace - CoreValues - Authenticity

To gain specific actions that a team can undertake to fully embrace and exemplify their core values, leading to significant and lasting change.

As a **Leadership Development Consultant**, adopting a **motivational and encouraging tone**, could you provide specific steps that **my team** can take to ensure they fully **embrace and exemplify their core values in a way that brings about significant and lasting change**? This is particularly relevant given the goal of **fostering a culture of integrity and authenticity within the team**.

As a **[profession]**, adopting a **[tone of voice]**, could you provide specific steps that **[my/their]** **[team/group/department]** can take to ensure they fully **[contextual challenge/opportunity]**? This is particularly relevant given the goal of **[desired outcome]**.

Example 1: As a Team Coach, adopting an inspiring and supportive tone, could you provide specific steps that my sales team can take to ensure they fully embrace and exemplify their core values in a way that brings about significant and lasting change? This is particularly relevant given the goal of fostering a culture of honesty and transparency within the sales team.

Example 2: As a Corporate Trainer, adopting a motivational and encouraging tone, could you provide specific steps that their customer service department can take to ensure they fully embrace and exemplify their core values in a way that brings about significant and lasting change? This is particularly relevant given the goal of fostering a culture of empathy and understanding within the customer service department.

PROMPT No 105

Tags

Self-awareness - ValuesAlignment - EthicalDecision

Goal

To provide leaders with a structured process to introspectively examine the alignment between their behavior and values in different situations. This self-exploration aims to elevate awareness, accountability, and ultimately the integrity with which leaders operate, leading to more authentic and effective leadership.

Prompt

As an **Executive Coach** with specialization in **values alignment and ethical decision-making** for the **technology industry**, could you guide me through **a self-assessment process to identify situations where I might not be honoring my values**? Include **introspective techniques, examples of scenarios that could be problematic, strategies for reconciliation, and action steps for realignment**. Ensure that the guide covers **how to integrate this self-awareness into my daily routine and strategic decisions**. Introduce unique angles and future implications. Let's think about this step by step. Write using an **informative** tone and **factual** writing style.

Formula

As a **[profession]** with specialization in **[focus area]** for the **[industry],** could you guide me through **[contextual challenge/opportunity]**? Include **[methods/techniques]**. Ensure that the guide covers **[tools/frameworks]**. Introduce unique angles and future implications. Let's think about this step by step. Write using a **[type]** tone and **[style]** writing style.

Examples

Example 1: As a Life Coach focusing on self-awareness for individuals in the creative arts, could you assist me in identifying the points at which my actions may diverge from my core values of creativity, integrity, and community? Include techniques like journaling prompts, examples of common value conflicts in the arts, and steps for resolving these conflicts. Make sure the guide offers suggestions for regular check-ins with myself or accountability partners. Incorporate unique angles like the role of values in creative expression. Let's dissect this carefully. Write using a personal tone and an empathic writing style.

Example 2: As a Leadership Consultant with a specialization in ethical alignment for the healthcare industry, could you help me discern the situations where I might compromise my values of patient care, innovation, and transparency? Include diagnostic questionnaires, real-world case studies from healthcare, and pathways for value alignment. Make sure the guide explains how to make this self-assessment a part of annual performance reviews or team discussions. Explore unique angles like bioethics considerations in value alignment. Let's break this down methodically. Write using a scholarly tone and a rigorous writing style.

PROMPT No 106

Tags

Consequences - Ethical - Assessment

To introspectively assess the repercussions or detriments stemming from the disregard of personal values, thereby fostering a deeper understanding and prompting corrective actions to realign behaviors and decisions with those values.

Prompt

Act as an **Ethical Leadership Consultant** with a specialization in **Value-Driven Decision Making** within the **financial services industry**. Could you guide me through **a reflective process to gauge the costs or consequences of continuing to overlook my values**? Please include **self-assessment tools, analytical frameworks, and reflective exercises**. Make sure to cover how **to measure the impact on personal and professional life, and how to initiate a dialogue about value alignment within my team**. Delve into **pioneering methodologies and alternative perspectives to reveal hidden costs and foster a value-centric culture**. Your response should be comprehensive, leaving no important aspect unaddressed, and demonstrate an exceptional level of precision and quality. Let's think about this step by step. Write using a **contemplative** tone and an **actionable** writing style.

Formula

Act as a **[profession]** with a specialization in **[area of expertise]** within the **[industry]**. Could you guide me through **[specific challenge/opportunity]**? Please include **[methods/techniques]**. Make sure to cover how **[key areas/topics]**. Delve into **[additional exploration]**. Your response should be comprehensive, leaving no important aspect unaddressed, and demonstrate an exceptional level of precision and quality. Let's think about this step by step. Write using a **[type]** tone and a **[style]** writing style.

Examples

Example 1: Act as a Personal Development Coach with a specialization in Value Clarification within the education sector. Could you guide me through a self-reflective journey to understand the costs or consequences of persistently ignoring my values? Please include self-discovery exercises, impact analysis frameworks, and strategies to realign actions with values. Make sure to cover how to evaluate the effect on relationships and job satisfaction, and how to promote value-driven discussions within my community. Traverse through innovative approaches and diverse viewpoints to unearth overlooked repercussions and advocate a values-aligned lifestyle. Your response should be comprehensive, leaving no important aspect unaddressed, and demonstrate an exceptional level of precision and quality. Let's think about this step by step. Write using an introspective tone and a transformative writing style.

Example 2: Act as a Corporate Ethicist with a specialization in Organizational Value Systems within the pharmaceutical industry. Could you guide me through an analytical exploration to ascertain the costs or consequences of continually sidelining my values? Please include ethical assessment tools, consequential analysis frameworks, and facilitated discussion guides. Make sure to cover how to quantify the impact on ethical climate and organizational reputation, and how to engage in value-centric dialogues within my team. Venture into groundbreaking paradigms and alternate viewpoints to expose hidden costs and foster ethical congruence. Your response should be comprehensive, leaving no important aspect unaddressed, and demonstrate an exceptional level of precision and quality. Let's think about this step by step. Write using a discerning tone and an evaluative writing style.

PROMPT No 107

Tags

SelfAwareness - Decision - Values

To obtain a comprehensive, actionable framework for reflecting on what it means to take actions aligned with one's personal values. The aim is to enhance self-awareness, facilitate value-based decision-making, and foster personal and professional growth.

As a **Personal Values Coach** in the **consulting industry**, could you provide a **comprehensive strategy** for reflecting on what it means for **me** to take actions that are aligned with **my** personal values? Additionally, offer **actionable steps** for **value-based decision-making**. Segment your insights into distinct modules, each supported by **evidence from reputable journals**. Investigate unexpected avenues and creative pathways. Let's dissect this carefully step by step. Write using a **contemplative** tone and a **nuanced** writing style.

As a **[profession]** in the **[industry]**, could you provide a **[comprehensive strategy/thorough toolkit/detailed blueprint]** for reflecting on what it means for **[me/us/them]** to take actions that are aligned with **[my/our/their]** personal values? Additionally, offer **[actionable steps/initial measures/immediate tactics]** for **[value-based decision-making/ethical choices/value-aligned actions]**. Segment your insights into distinct modules, each supported by **[evidence from/references from/data from]** **[reputable journals/credible research/authoritative publications]**. Investigate unexpected avenues and creative pathways. Let's dissect this carefully step by step. Write using a **[contemplative/reflective/insightful]** tone and a **[nuanced/engaging/innovative]** writing style.

Example 1: As a Life Coach in the healthcare sector, could you provide a detailed blueprint outlining the methods for reflecting on what it means for a medical professional to take actions that are aligned with their personal values? Additionally, offer initial measures for ethical choices. Segment your insights into distinct modules, each authenticated by corroborative evidence from credible sources. Explore unconventional approaches and diverse viewpoints. Let's examine each dimension meticulously. Write using a reflective tone and an engaging writing style.

Example 2: As a Career Development Consultant in the arts sector, could you provide a thorough toolkit outlining the strategies an artist can use for reflecting on what it means to take actions that are aligned with their personal values? Additionally, offer immediate tactics for value-based decision-making. Segment your insights into distinct modules, each endorsed with data from verified academic publications. Unearth hidden gems and non-traditional methods. Let's dissect this carefully. Write using a contemplative tone and an innovative writing style.

WEAKNESS

PROMPT No 108

WeaknessAcknowledgment - Team - SelfAwareness

To acquire a comprehensive, actionable framework for guiding a team in reflecting on the degree to which they acknowledge and accept their weaknesses, aiming to foster self-awareness, team cohesion, and overall performance improvement.

As a **Self-Awareness Coach** in the **education sector**, could you offer a **comprehensive roadmap** outlining the aspects I should consider when guiding **my team** in reflecting on the degree to which they acknowledge and accept their **weaknesses**? Please include **both self-assessment questionnaires and group discussion guidelines**. Segment the guide into distinct categories, each supported by **evidence from reputable journals**. Explore unconventional approaches and diverse viewpoints. Let's tackle this in a phased manner. Write using a **balanced** tone and a **narrative** writing style.

As a **[profession]** in the **[industry]**, could you offer a **[thorough toolkit/comprehensive roadmap/detailed blueprint]** outlining the aspects **[I/Name/Role]** should consider when guiding **[my/our/their]** **[team/group/department]** in reflecting on the degree to which they acknowledge and accept their **[weaknesses/strengths/limitations]**? Please include both **[self-assessment questionnaires/group discussion guidelines/reflective exercises]**. Segment the guide into distinct categories, each supported by **[evidence from/references from/data from]** **[reputable journals/credible research/authoritative publications]**. Explore unconventional approaches and diverse viewpoints. Let's tackle this in a phased manner. Write using a **[balanced/empathetic/consultative]** tone and a **[narrative/nuanced/concise]** writing style.

Example 1: As a Team Development Specialist in the healthcare sector, could you offer a comprehensive roadmap outlining the aspects a nursing team should consider when reflecting on the degree to which they acknowledge and accept their weaknesses? Please include both self-assessment scales and facilitated group dialogues. Segment the guide into distinct categories, each authenticated by corroborative evidence from credible sources. Investigate unexpected avenues and creative pathways. Let's examine each dimension meticulously. Write using a focused tone and a nuanced writing style.

Example 2: As an Organizational Psychologist in the finance industry, could you offer a detailed blueprint outlining the aspects an investment team should consider when reflecting on the degree to which they acknowledge and accept their weaknesses? Please include both psychometric tests and team-building exercises. Segment the guide into distinct categories, each endorsed with data from verified sources. Unearth hidden gems and non-traditional methods. Let's tackle this in a phased manner. Write using an empathetic tone and a concise writing style.

PROMPT No 109

Action-Plan - Emotional-Intelligence - Improvement

To obtain a detailed and comprehensive action plan outlining the specific steps that a team can undertake to effectively address and enhance a weakness related to a lack of emotional intelligence or any other weakness.

As a **Leadership Development Consultant**, adopting a **supportive and encouraging tone**, could you provide a detailed and comprehensive action plan outlining the specific steps that **my team** can undertake to effectively address and enhance a weakness related to **a lack of emotional intelligence or any other weakness**? This is particularly relevant given the goal of **fostering a culture of continuous learning and improvement within the team**.

As a **[profession]**, adopting a **[tone of voice]**, could you provide a detailed and comprehensive action plan outlining the specific steps that **[my/their]** **[team/group/department]** can undertake to effectively address and enhance a weakness related to **[contextual challenge/opportunity]**? This is particularly relevant given the goal of **[desired outcome]**.

Example 1: As a Human Resources Consultant, adopting a supportive and encouraging tone, could you provide a detailed and comprehensive action plan outlining the specific steps that my sales team can undertake to effectively address and enhance a weakness related to a lack of emotional intelligence? This is particularly relevant given the goal of fostering a culture of continuous learning and improvement within the sales team.

Example 2: As a Team Coach, adopting a supportive and encouraging tone, could you provide a detailed and comprehensive action plan outlining the specific steps that the marketing department can undertake to effectively address and enhance a weakness related to a lack of communication skills? This is particularly relevant given the goal of fostering a culture of continuous learning and improvement within the marketing department.

PROMPT No 110

Opportunities - Discussion - Strengths

To design an effective strategy for business leaders to facilitate conversations with their teams on how perceived weaknesses could have positive payoffs if enhanced. This would lead to increased productivity, stronger team unity, and overall growth on both personal and professional fronts.

As a **Leadership Development Coach** with specialization in **team effectiveness** for the **technology industry**, could you guide me through the **strategy of holding a compelling conversation with my team to explore the concept that their perceived weaknesses may actually be opportunities for growth with the right focus and effort**? Please include **tips for initiating the dialogue, types of questions that can lead to insightful responses, methods to ensure an environment conducive** for **open discussion, and steps for post-discussion action plans that aim at capitalizing on these newfound opportunities**. Ensure that the guide covers **techniques to encourage self-assessment and peer-to-peer reviews**. Introduce unique angles and prophetic opportunities. Let's think about this step by step. Write using an **informative** tone and **factual** writing style.

As a **[profession]** with specialization in **[topic/specialization]** for the **[industry]**, could you guide me through the **[contextual challenge/opportunity]**? Please include **[methods/techniques/steps]** for **[specific aspects]**. Ensure that the guide covers [aspects/topics to be covered]. Introduce unique angles and prophetic opportunities. Let's think about this step by step. Write using a [type] tone and [style] writing style.

Examples

Example 1: As a Human Resources Advisor with a focus on Talent Management for the retail industry, could you guide me through initiating a productive conversation with my team to explore the notion that their perceived weaknesses may actually be growth opportunities? Include strategies for setting the stage, questions aimed at introspection, and techniques to foster a safe environment for discussion. Elaborate on post-discussion action plans that focus on turning weaknesses into strengths. Be sure the guide includes self-assessment methods like the SWOT analysis and tools for peer-to-peer reviews. Introduce revolutionary ideas and futuristic possibilities. Let's break this down systematically. Write using a professional tone and factual writing style.

Example 2: As an Organizational Psychologist with a specialization in Behavioral Economics, could you guide me through the strategy of opening a discourse with my team to discuss how their perceived weaknesses could be beneficial if improved? Incorporate methods to start the dialogue, the kinds of questions that trigger self-exploration, ways to ensure a psychologically safe space, and action steps for individual and team growth. Make sure the guide emphasizes the importance of metrics and peer-to-peer evaluations. Illuminate advanced techniques and transformative insights. Let's analyze this intricately. Write using an analytical tone and precise writing style.

PROMPT No 111

Tags

Evaluation - Skills - Productivity

Goal

To gain specific tactics or methods that can be utilized to thoroughly evaluate a team's weaknesses and pinpoint areas where they can improve their skills or knowledge.

Prompt

As a **Leadership Development Consultant**, adopting a **solution-oriented tone**, could you provide specific tactics or methods that **I** can utilize to thoroughly evaluate **my team's weaknesses and pinpoint areas where they can improve their skills or knowledge**? This is particularly relevant given the goal of **enhancing team performance and productivity**.

Formula

As a **[profession]**, adopting a **[tone of voice]**, could you provide specific tactics or methods that **[I/Name/Role]** can utilize to thoroughly evaluate **[my/their] [team/group/department]'s [contextual challenge/opportunity]**? This is particularly relevant given the goal of **[desired outcome]**.

Examples

Example 1: As a Human Resources Consultant, adopting a constructive tone, could you provide specific tactics or methods that a department head can utilize to thoroughly evaluate their faculty's weaknesses and pinpoint areas where they can improve their skills or knowledge? This is particularly relevant given the goal of enhancing academic performance and productivity.

Example 2: As a Team Coach, adopting an encouraging tone, could you provide specific tactics or methods that I can utilize to thoroughly evaluate my project team's weaknesses and pinpoint areas where they can improve their skills or knowledge? This is particularly relevant given the goal of enhancing project performance and productivity.

Final Words

In the domain of coaching, mentoring, and leadership, navigating the complexities requires a disciplined approach. This book aims to be an instrumental guide, leveraging artificial intelligence and prompt engineering to provide actionable insights for those in any profession. I have presented a curated list of prompts, each serving a specific objective: to clarify roles, define leadership strategies, and optimize coaching techniques, to name a few.

The scope of this book goes beyond a mere compilation of prompts. My goal is to impart a strategic mindset for interpreting challenges as opportunities, seeing barriers as milestones for growth, and viewing the future as a dynamic environment that can be strategically managed.

For the reader who began with skepticism, I hope you conclude this book with a newfound confidence, equipped with a toolkit that elevates your professional standing. For the experienced practitioner, may the methods and strategies here serve to refine your existing approaches.

This journey, while individual in nature, is set against the backdrop of collective human experience. Artificial intelligence serves as a bridge to this collective wisdom, streamlining the path toward your professional and personal development objectives.

In summary, this book aims to leave you not just prepared but empowered. As you close this chapter and move forward in your career, be reminded that each decision and action point offers an opportunity for growth and leadership. This is not just preparation; it is empowerment for transformative impact.

The challenges you face should be viewed as opportunities for demonstrating your leadership and expertise. I encourage you to approach these with a strategic focus, grounded in the knowledge and insights you have gained from this book.

I wish you all the best.

Mauricio

PS: Enjoyed your book? Scan the QR code to quickly leave a review. Thank you!

APPENDIXES

Appendix No 1

Sign-In to Chatbots

1,1. Chat GPT

Step 1: Visit ChatGPT on https://chat.openai.com/chat Click on "Sign Up" and then create your account.

Step 2: Verify your Account. You'd have to enter your details, verify your email and give an OTP you'll receive on your phone.

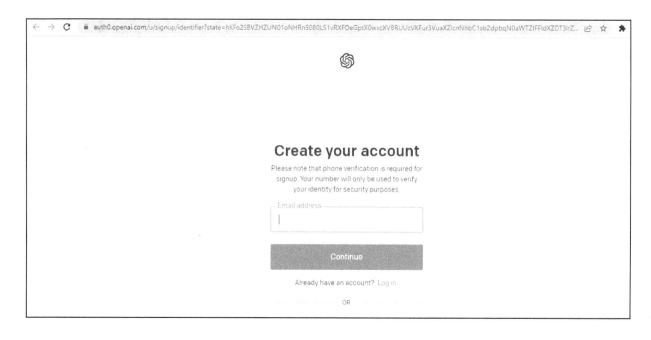

Once done, you'd have access to the free version of ChatGPT

As of April 2023, ChatGPT 3.5 is free to use and ChatGPT-4 costs $20 per month. As a beginner, you can easily test your skills on the free version.

This is how it looks:

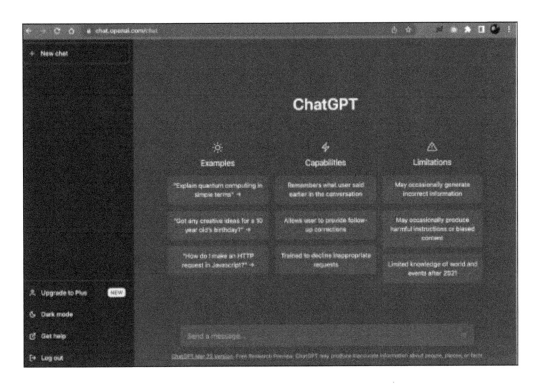

At the very bottom is where you'd chat:

You can now ask GPT anything you want, and it'll give you the desired result

Note: The procedure outlined was developed based on the instructions available at the time of writing. If you require further assistance with signing up for ChatGPT, please scan this QR code:

1.2. Bing Chat

Step 1: Go to the Microsoft website (www.microsoft.com).

Locate the download page for Edge or look for "Microsoft Edge" in the search bar. If you don't want to download Microsoft Edge, go directly to Step 6. For better results, we recommend using Microsoft Edge.

Step 2: Click the download button and choose the version that fits your system.

Step 3: Once downloaded, open the setup file.

Step 4: A User Account Control dialog box will appear – click "Yes" to grant permission.

The installation wizard will guide you through a series of prompts and options. Review them carefully.

Step 5: To open Microsfot Edge, press Win + R on the keyboard to open the Run window. In the Open field, type "microsoft-edge:" and press Enter on the keyboard or click or tap OK. Microsoft Edge is now open.

Step 6: Head to bing.com/chat

Step 7: From the pop-up that appears, click 'Start chatting'

Step 8: Enter the email address for the Microsoft account you'd like to use and click 'Next'.

If you don't have one, click 'Create one!' just under the text box and follow the instructions. Enter your password when prompted and click Next. From the following screen, choose whether you'd like to stay signed in or not. Click 'Chat Now'

Step 9: Choose your conversation style. If you've never used it before, it's best to stick with 'More Balanced'

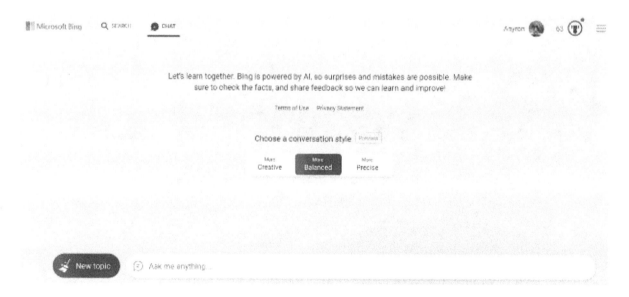

That's it! You can now start chatting.

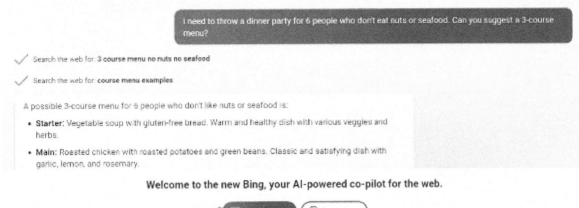

Chat mode is only available when you have access to the new Bing.

I need to throw a dinner party for 6 people who don't eat nuts or seafood. Can you suggest a 3-course menu?

✓ Search the web for: 3 course menu no nuts no seafood

✓ Search the web for: course menu examples

A possible 3-course menu for 6 people who don't like nuts or seafood is:

- **Starter:** Vegetable soup with gluten-free bread. Warm and healthy dish with various veggies and herbs.
- **Main:** Roasted chicken with roasted potatoes and green beans. Classic and satisfying dish with garlic, lemon, and rosemary.

Welcome to the new Bing, your AI-powered co-pilot for the web.

Note: The procedure outlined was developed based on the instructions available at the time of writing. If you require assistance with signing up for Bing Chat, please scan this QR code:

1.3. Google Bard

Step 1: Go to bard.google.com. Select Try Bard. Accept Google Bard Terms of Service

Step 2: Go to "Sign in"

Step 3: Enter a query or search term and then hit enter.

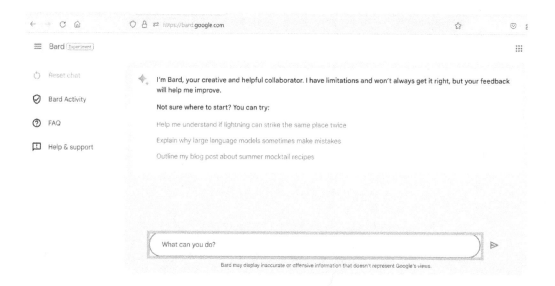

Wait for the AI to respond. You can then either continue the conversation or select Google It to use the traditional search engine.

Note: The procedure outlined was developed based on the instructions available at the time of writing. If you require assistance with signing up for Google Bard, please scan this QR code:

1.4. Meta LLaMA

Getting the Models

Step 1: Go to https://ai.meta.com/resources/models-and-libraries/llama-downloads/

Step 2: Fill the form with your information.

Step 3: Accept their license (if you agree with it)

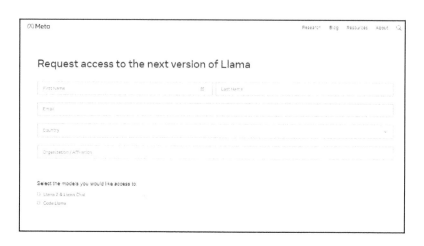

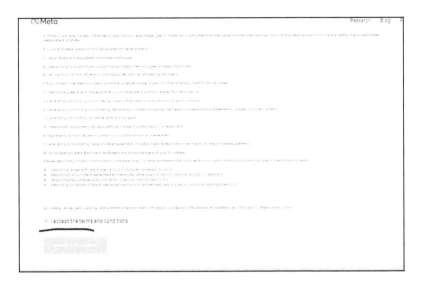

Step 4: Once your request is approved, you will receive a signed URL over email.

Step 5: Clone the Llama 2 repository (go to https://github.com/facebookresearch/llama).

Step 6: Run the download.sh script, passing the URL provided when prompted to start the download. Keep in mind that the links expire after 24 hours and a certain amount of downloads. If you start seeing errors such as 403: Forbidden, you can always re-request a link.

<u>Appendix No 2</u>

Follow-up Prompts

There are 1100 prompts that you can use as follow-ups in order to get more specific or revised information from ChatGPT and other Chatbots. Don't forget to tailor these prompts to your specific circumstances and to the response you previously received from the Chatbot.

Each of these prompt types serves a different purpose and can be used effectively in different scenarios. Depending on the context and the intended outcome, one type of prompt may be more suitable than another.

These prompts are divided into eleven distinct categories, each tailored to specific conversational needs: Generic, Enhancement, Clarification, Probing, Critical Thinking, Instructional, Exploration, Comparison, Summarization, Evaluation, and Hypothetical.

To have access to 1100 follow-up prompts, please scan this QR code:

Appendix No 3

A Beginner's Step-by-Step Guide to Using ChatGPT

If you're new to ChatGPT, don't fret. This guide is designed to walk you through its use, step by step. By the end, you'll have a solid grasp of how to harness the power of this incredible tool.

Step 1: Accessing the Platform

Visit OpenAI's Platform: Head to OpenAI's official website: ChatGPT [openai.com]

Sign Up/Log In: If you don't have an account, you'll need to sign up. If you already have one, simply log in.

Step 2: Navigating the Interface

Dashboard: This is your central hub, where you can access various tools and see your usage stats.

Start a New Session: To interact with ChatGPT, start a new session or use a predefined platform depending on the current interface.

Step 3: Interacting with ChatGPT

Input Field: This is where you'll type or paste the prompts from our book.

Submit: Once you've entered your prompt, press 'Enter' or click the 'Submit' button.

Review Output: ChatGPT will generate a response. Take a moment to read and understand it.

Step 4: Refining Your Interaction

Being Specific: If you need specific information or a particular type of response, make your prompts more detailed.

Iterate: If the first response isn't what you're looking for, tweak your prompt and try again.

Step 5: Utilizing the Prompts from This Book

Choose a Prompt: Browse the book's prompt section and select one that aligns with your current needs.

Input: Copy and paste or type the chosen prompt into ChatGPT's input field.

Customization: Feel free to adjust the prompts to be more specific to your situation.

Step 6: Safety and Best Practices

Sensitive Information: Never share sensitive personal information, such as Social Security numbers or bank details, with ChatGPT or any online platform.

Understanding Outputs: Remember, while ChatGPT can produce human-like responses, it doesn't understand context in the same way humans do. Always review its advice with a critical eye.

Step 7: Exploring Advanced Features

As you become more comfortable with ChatGPT:

Experiment: Play around with different types of prompts to see the diverse responses you can get.

Integrate with Other Tools: There are several third-party tools and platforms that have integrated ChatGPT. Explore these to maximize your work.

Step 8: Stay Updated

Technology, especially in the AI field, evolves rapidly. Periodically check OpenAI's official channels for updates, new features, or changes to the platform.

By following this guide, even the most tech-averse individuals will find themselves comfortably navigating and interacting with ChatGPT. As we delve deeper into the book and introduce specific prompts tailored for your work you'll be equipped with the knowledge to make the most of them.

Here is our "*Elevate Your Productivity Using ChatGPT*" Guide: To access this guide to boost your efficiency and productivity, please scan this QR code.

Appendix No 4

Mentoring, Coaching, and Leadership Professionals

This list encompasses professions pivotal in nurturing growth, leadership, and collaboration in work settings. They play crucial roles in guiding, training, and inspiring individuals towards achieving personal and organizational objectives.

1. Mentor: Provides guidance, support, and wisdom to less experienced individuals for personal and professional growth.
2. Coach: Assists in developing specific skills, improving performance, and achieving defined objectives through structured guidance.
3. Leader: Guides, inspires, and influences a group towards achieving common goals, fostering positive organizational culture.
4. Executive Coach: Assists executives in honing leadership skills, achieving goals, and navigating career transitions.
5. Life Coach: Guides individuals in personal development, goal-setting, and achieving life balance.
6. Career Counselor: Provides advice on career exploration, development strategies, and job search.
7. Organizational Consultant: Aids organizations in improving performance, culture, and change management.
8. Training and Development Manager: Plans, directs, and coordinates programs to enhance employee skills.
9. Human Resources Manager: Oversees recruitment, employee relations, and organizational development.
10. Management Consultant: Advises on business strategies, problem-solving, and organizational improvements.
11. Leadership Development Specialist: Creates programs to develop leadership capabilities within organizations.
12. Performance Coach: Helps individuals improve performance and achieve professional objectives.
13. Business Coach: Guides entrepreneurs in business growth, strategy, and problem-solving.
14. Conflict Resolution Specialist: Aids in resolving disputes and improving communication in workplaces.
15. Executive Search Consultant: Assists organizations in identifying and recruiting executive leadership talent.
16. Team Building Specialist: Designs and facilitates activities to enhance team cohesion.
17. Corporate Trainer: Provides training to improve employee skills and knowledge.
18. Sales Trainer: Develops and delivers training programs to improve sales team performance and effectiveness.
19. Communication Coach: Improves interpersonal communication skills within professional settings.
20. Change Management Consultant: Guides organizations through change with strategies to ensure smooth transitions.
21. Culture Development Consultant: Aids in cultivating a positive, productive organizational culture.
22. Educational Consultant: Advises on educational strategies, curriculum development, and leadership.
23. Talent Development Specialist: Identifies and nurtures employee talents for organizational growth.
24. Learning and Development Specialist: Designs and implements training programs to promote employee growth and organizational success.
25. Supply Chain Manager: Oversees the end-to-end supply chain process to ensure efficiency and effectiveness.

26. Negotiation Consultant: Aids in enhancing negotiation skills and strategies.
27. Mediator: Facilitates resolution of disputes in a neutral manner.
28. Process Improvement Consultant: Aids in enhancing operational processes for greater efficiency and productivity.
29. Employee Engagement Consultant: Boosts employee satisfaction and productivity through engagement strategies.
30. Entrepreneurship Advisor: Guides individuals in launching and growing their own businesses.

Appendix No 5

Specializations for Mentors, Coaches and Leaders

1. This compilation presents specialized roles integral to fostering excellence, innovation, and resilience within professional landscapes, offering tailored guidance and support to propel individuals and businesses toward their aspirations.
2. Leadership: Enhancing skills for leading teams and organizations effectively.
3. Performance: Boosting individual or team productivity and output.
4. Career: Navigating career progression and transitions.
5. Sales: Increasing sales proficiency and results.
6. Marketing: Crafting and executing marketing strategies.
7. Strategy: Formulating and applying long-term business plans.
8. Innovation: Fostering creative thinking and new ideas.
9. Culture: Shaping positive organizational values and practices.
10. Conflict Resolution: Managing and resolving disputes effectively.
11. Communication Skills: Improving sharing and receiving of information.
12. Emotional Intelligence: Understanding and managing emotions for improved interactions.
13. Team Dynamics: Strengthening team cooperation and function.
14. Change Leadership: Guiding successful organizational change.
15. Diversity and Inclusion: Building respectful, diverse work environments.
16. Work-Life Balance: Balancing professional responsibilities with personal life.
17. Organizational Development: Enhancing organizational structures and efficiency.
18. Time Management: Prioritizing tasks and managing time wisely.
19. Customer Success: Ensuring clients achieve their desired outcomes.
20. Personal Branding: Crafting and communicating a personal image.
21. Corporate Governance: Directing company management and policies.
22. Business Ethics: Promoting ethical professional conduct.
23. Financial Coaching for Executives: Managing company finances and economic strategy.
24. Talent Development: Growing employee skills and career paths.
25. Digital Transformation: Integrating digital technology into all business areas.
26. Entrepreneurship: Starting and growing new business ventures.
27. Global Leadership: Leading across diverse cultures and markets.
28. Sustainability Leadership: Integrating eco-friendly practices into business.
29. Crisis Leadership: Leading effectively through emergencies.
30. Mindfulness and Well-being: Promoting mental health and mindfulness practices.

Appendix No 6

Tones

Tone reflects the emotional stance towards the subject or audience, impacting engagement and receptivity. In coaching or leadership, the right tone fosters trust, motivation, and effective communication, aligning with growth-oriented goals.

1. Motivational: Inspiring action and positivity towards achieving goals.
2. Empathetic: Demonstrating understanding and compassion towards others' experiences.
3. Authoritative: Exuding confidence and expertise in guiding others.
4. Inspirational: Provoking thought and encouraging higher aspirations.
5. Supportive: Offering encouragement and backing during challenges.
6. Reflective: Encouraging contemplation and self-assessment.
7. Directive: Providing clear, actionable guidance.
8. Analytical: Examining situations critically and logically.
9. Advisory: Offering suggestions based on expertise.
10. Challenging: Encouraging stretching beyond comfort zones.
11. Respectful: Honoring individuals' values, thoughts, and feelings.
12. Humorous: Adding levity to engage and ease tension.
13. Socratic: Encouraging critical thinking through questioning.
14. Constructive: Providing feedback for growth and improvement.
15. Patient: Showing understanding and tolerance during learning processes.
16. Optimistic: Highlighting the positive and potential success.
17. Realistic: Providing a practical and sensible perspective.
18. Encouraging: Boosting morale and self-efficacy.
19. Appreciative: Acknowledging efforts and achievements.
20. Reassuring: Alleviating concerns and instilling confidence.
21. Inquisitive: Encouraging exploration and curiosity.
22. Observational: Noting and reflecting on behaviors and outcomes.
23. Persuasive: Convincing others towards a certain viewpoint.
24. Resilient: Demonstrating toughness and adaptability in adversity.
25. Visionary: Focusing on long-term potential and broader horizons.
26. Collegial: Promoting a sense of partnership and teamwork.
27. Energizing: Infusing enthusiasm and vigor.
28. Compassionate: Showing care and understanding in dealing with others.
29. Professional: Maintaining a formal and respectful demeanor.
30. Mindful: Demonstrating awareness and consideration.

Appendix No 7

Writing Styles

Writing style denotes how ideas are expressed, encompassing word choice and narrative flow. In coaching, mentoring, and leadership, an apt style clarifies concepts, provides guidance, and facilitates meaningful exploration of ideas.

1. Expository: Explaining facts and information clearly and straightforwardly.
2. Descriptive: Painting a vivid picture to convey a particular scenario or idea.
3. Narrative: Telling a story or recounting events to convey lessons or insights.
4. Persuasive: Arguing a point or encouraging a particular action or mindset.
5. Concise: Delivering information in a brief, direct manner.
6. Analytical: Dissecting information to understand and convey underlying principles.
7. Reflective: Encouraging introspection and consideration of past experiences.
8. Dialogic: Engaging in a two-way conversation to explore ideas.
9. Illustrative: Using examples and anecdotes to clarify points.
10. Instructive: Providing detailed guidance or instructions.
11. Interpretive: Explaining and making sense of complex concepts.
12. Comparative: Analyzing similarities and differences between concepts.
13. Argumentative: Making a case for a particular stance or action.
14. Problem-Solution: Identifying issues and proposing solutions.
15. Evaluative: Assessing the value or effectiveness of certain practices.
16. Journalistic: Reporting facts in an objective, straightforward manner.
17. Exploratory: Delving into topics to discover new insights or perspectives.
18. Contemplative: Encouraging deep thought on certain topics.
19. Case Study: Delving into real-world examples to extract lessons.
20. Research-based: Grounding discourse in empirical evidence.
21. Informal: Adopting a casual, accessible approach.
22. Formal: Adhering to professional language and structure.
23. Technical: Utilizing specialized terminology relevant to the field.
24. Conceptual: Exploring ideas at a high level.
25. Practical: Focusing on actionable advice and real-world application.
26. Empirical: Relying on observation and experience.
27. Theoretical: Delving into theories and abstract concepts.
28. Storyboard: Unfolding ideas through a sequenced narrative.
29. Interactive: Encouraging active engagement from the reader.
30. Scenario-based: Outlining hypothetical situations to explore concepts.

Appendix No 8

Tags

	Chapter	Tag 1	Tag 2	Tag 3
Prompt 1	Accountability	Engagement	Virtual Environment	Team Presence
Prompt 2	Accountability	Courage Enhancement	Risk-Taking	Innovative Culture
Prompt 3	Accountability	Strategic Planning	Competitive Advantage	Team Performance
Prompt 4	Accountability	Self-Discovery	Personal Development	Strengths
Prompt 5	Accountability	Decision-Making	Bold Choices	Informed Analysis
Prompt 6	Awareness	Emotional Intelligence	Fear Addressing	Team Morale
Prompt 7	Awareness	Personal Growth	Achievement Strategies	Individual Development
Prompt 8	Awareness	Role Visualization	Value Articulation	Sense of Belonging
Prompt 9	Awareness	Thought Awareness	Responsibility Management	Interaction Impact
Prompt 10	Awareness	Recognition	Beliefs	Management
Prompt 11	Awareness	Empathy	Emotion	Interpretation
Prompt 12	Belief	Counter-evidence	Critical-Thinking	Evaluation
Prompt 13	Belief	Assumptions	Conflict	Resolution
Prompt 14	Belief	Contradiction	Values	Resolution
Prompt 15	Belief	Satisfaction	Fulfillment	Communication
Prompt 16	Belief	Transformation	Assumptions	Facilitation
Prompt 17	Belief	Belief	Motivation	Action
Prompt 18	Challenge	Career	Assistance	Progression
Prompt 19	Challenge	Diversity	Problem-Solving	Strategies
Prompt 20	Challenge	Resilience	Problem-Solving	Empowerment
Prompt 21	Challenge	Learning	Mistakes	Growth
Prompt 22	Challenge	Communication	HR	Obstacle-Resolution
Prompt 23	Change	Relationship-Building	Collaboration	Work-Environment
Prompt 24	Change	Future-Readiness	Leadership	Perspective-Shift
Prompt 25	Change	Evaluation	Consequence	Work-Methods
Prompt 26	Commitment	Motivation	Ownership	Vision
Prompt 27	Commitment	Dedication	Strategy	Goal-Progress
Prompt 28	Creativity	Self-Assessment	Evaluation	Improvement
Prompt 29	Creativity	Creativity	Innovation	Strategy
Prompt 30	Decisions	Productivity	Time-Management	Prioritization
Prompt 31	Decisions	Quality	Motivation	Environment
Prompt 32	Excitement	Motivation	Excitement	Strategy
Prompt 33	Excitement	CSR	Employee-Involvement	Brand-Reputation
Prompt 34	Excitement	Communication	Harmony	Openness
Prompt 35	Fear	Transparency	Communication	Support
Prompt 36	Fear	Self-Criticism	Potential	Identification
Prompt 37	Feelings	Information-Gathering	Emotions	Tactfulness
Prompt 38	Feelings	Self-Awareness	Empowerment	Bias
Prompt 39	Flow	Focus	Evaluation	Effort
Prompt 40	Flow	Communication	Inner-Self	Professional-Growth

Prompt 41	Fulfillment	Monotony	Enhancement	Boredom
Prompt 42	Fulfillment	Exemplary	Boss	Effectiveness
Prompt 43	Goals	Synchronization	Learning	Objectives
Prompt 44	Goals	Prioritization	Goals	Alignment
Prompt 45	Goals	Learning	Engagement	Objectives
Prompt 46	Goals	Leadership	Conversations	Alignment
Prompt 47	Habits	Self-Sabotage	Transportation	Leadership
Prompt 48	Habits	Engagement	Meetings	Incentivize
Prompt 49	Learning	Assessment	Opportunities	Methodologies
Prompt 50	Learning	Introspection	Conversations	Improvement
Prompt 51	Learning	Problem-solving	Communication	Safety
Prompt 52	Learning	LearningCulture	Innovation	Insurance
Prompt 53	Learning	Facilitation	Reflection	Assessment
Prompt 54	Learning	Reflection	Sacrifices	Outcomes
Prompt 55	Learning	Understanding	Motivation	Alignment
Prompt 56	Listenning	Resilience	Discussion	Failure
Prompt 57	Mindset	Self-Reflection	Growth	FinTech
Prompt 58	Mindset	Mindset	Professionalism	Self-Reflection
Prompt 59	Mindset	Growth-Mindset	Resilience	Learning
Prompt 60	Mindset	Self-Awareness	Performance	Optimization
Prompt 61	Mindset	Purpose	Engagement	Mission
Prompt 62	Options	Decision-Making	Analysis	Strategy
Prompt 63	Options	Appreciation	Feedback	Listening
Prompt 64	Options	Organizational-Behavior	Empathy	Motivation
Prompt 65	Performance	Recognition	Team-Dynamics	Tech
Prompt 66	Performance	Obstacles	Self-Improvement	Introspection
Prompt 67	Performance	Benefits	Organizational-Psychology	Tech
Prompt 68	Preferences	CognitivePsychology	Behavioral	DecisionMaking
Prompt 69	Priorities	TimeManagement	Strategies	Priorities
Prompt 70	Priorities	Team-Management	Empathy	Satisfaction
Prompt 71	Progress	Inspiration	Alignment	Potential
Prompt 72	Progress	Satisfaction	Evaluation	Motivation
Prompt 73	Purpose	Consciousness	Alignment	Leadership
Prompt 74	Purpose	Metrics	Criteria	Quantitative
Prompt 75	Purpose	Interpersonal	Inquiry	Non-Verbal
Prompt 76	Purpose	Cohesion	Purpose	Reflection
Prompt 77	Relationships	Trust	Assessment	Collaboration
Prompt 78	Relationships	Selection	Software	Team-building
Prompt 79	Relationships	Presence	Mindfulness	Contemplative
Prompt 80	Relationships	Resourcefulness	Strategy	Human Resources
Prompt 81	Relationships	Relationships	Communication	Barriers
Prompt 82	Relationships	Motivation	Implementation	Satisfaction
Prompt 83	Relationships	Patience	Interactions	Self-Reflection
Prompt 84	Relationships	Empowerment	Self-efficacy	Motivation
Prompt 85	Relationships	Resources	Implementation	Performance
Prompt 86	Relationships	Futurist	Brainstorming	Innovation
Prompt 87	Self-assessment	Introspection	Decision-making	Behavior

Prompt 88	Self-assessment	Evolution	Mentoring	Perspectives
Prompt 89	Self-assessment	Feedback	Communication	Motivations
Prompt 90	Skills	Acquisition	Performance	Alignment
Prompt 91	Strategies	Recognition	Resilience	Acknowledgment
Prompt 92	Strategies	Effectiveness	ROI	Decision-making
Prompt 93	Strength	Attraction	Roles	Inherent
Prompt 94	Strength	Strengths	Productivity	Morale
Prompt 95	Strength	Development	Strengths	Metrics
Prompt 96	Strength	Strengths	Performance	Methodology
Prompt 97	Strength	Consequences	Strengths	Mitigation
Prompt 98	Strength	Optimization	Strengths	Stakeholders
Prompt 99	Strength	Opportunities	Skill-Gap	Metrics
Prompt 100	Support	Sales Targets	KPIs	Risk Mitigation
Prompt 101	Support	Work Arrangements	Team Survey	KPI Alignment
Prompt 102	Support	Strategy	Stakeholders	Collaboration
Prompt 103	Values	Values	Alignment	Communication
Prompt 104	Values	Embrace	CoreValues	Authenticity
Prompt 105	Values	Self-awareness	ValuesAlignment	EthicalDecision
Prompt 106	Values	Consequences	Ethical	Assessment
Prompt 107	Values	SelfAwareness	Decision	Values
Prompt 108	Weakness	WeaknessAcknowledgment	Team	SelfAwareness
Prompt 109	Weakness	Action-Plan	Emotional-Intelligence	Improvement
Prompt 110	Weakness	Opportunities	Discussion	Strengths
Prompt 111	Weakness	Evaluation	Skills	Productivity

Appendix No 9

Unlock the Full Potential of This Book - Instantly

Dive into a world of convenience with our electronic copy! Feel free to seamlessly copy and paste any prompt that sparks your interest.

Customize them to fit your unique needs. Say goodbye to the hassle of retyping. Start crafting your perfect prompts with ease and efficiency!.

To access the electronic copy, please scan this QR code:

www.ingramcontent.com/pod-product-compliance
Lightning Source LLC
LaVergne TN
LVHW082036050326
832904LV00005B/199